A Standard Operating Procedure for the Surgical Implantation of Transmitters in Juvenile Salmonids

By T.L. Liedtke, J.W. Beeman, and L.P. Gee

Open-File Report 2012–1267

U.S. Department of the Interior
U.S. Geological Survey

U.S. Department of the Interior
KEN SALAZAR, Secretary

U.S. Geological Survey
Marcia K. McNutt, Director

U.S. Geological Survey, Reston, Virginia: 2012

For more information on the USGS—the Federal source for science about the Earth,
its natural and living resources, natural hazards, and the environment—visit
http://www.usgs.gov or call 1–888–ASK–USGS

For an overview of USGS information products, including maps, imagery, and publications,
visit *http://www.usgs.gov/pubprod*

To order this and other USGS information products, visit *http://store.usgs.gov*

Suggested citation:
Liedtke, T.L., Beeman, J.W., and Gee, L.P., 2012, A standard operating procedure for the surgical implantation of
transmitters in juvenile salmonids: U.S. Geological Survey Open-File Report 2012-1267, 50 p.

Contents

Introduction 1

Purpose and Applicability 2

Guiding Principles 2

    Develop Surgical Proficiency 2

    Anticipate and Manage Tagger Effects 3

    Reduce and Refine Fish Handling 4

    Practice Aseptic Techniques 4

    Manage Anesthesia 6

    Construct an Effective Tagging Station 7

Procedures 10

    Fish Collection, Holding, and Transport 10

    Fish Size Criteria 14

    Tagging Preparations 14

    Anesthetizing Fish 17

    Measuring Fish Size 18

    Implantation of Transmitters 19

    Post-Tag Recovery 25

    Release of Tagged Fish 26

    Clean-Up and Disinfection 27

    Recommendations 27

        Maximize Efficiency 27

        Monitor and Document SOP Compliance 28

        Evaluate Transmitter Effects 28

        Report Methods in Detail 29

        Recapture Tagged Fish 29

Summary 29

Acknowledgments 30

References Cited 30

Appendix A: Materials Needed 35

Appendix B: Abbreviated Procedures 38

Appendix C: SOP Compliance Form 46

Figures

Figure 1. An example surgical platform constructed of acrylic glass 7

Figure 2. An example surgical platform consisting of closed-cell foam with sections carved to support the fish in proper surgical orientation 8

Figure 3. An example gravity feed irrigation system 9

Figure 4. An example tagging station with gravity feed irrigation system, instrument disinfection and rinse trays, and surgical platform 9

Figure 5. Holding tank with immersed 19-liter perforated recovery containers. 12

Figure 6. Example micro scalpel configurations. 15

Figure 7. A perforated 19-liter recovery container 16

Figure 8. Ventral view of a juvenile salmon on a tagging platform. 19

Figure 9. Lateral view of a juvenile salmon with location of structures and organs and approximate location of the surgical incision 20

Figure 10. Example catheters used to perform a shielded needle technique to create an exit location for a trailing antenna on a radio transmitter 21

Figure 11. Lateral, external view of a juvenile salmon with the location for the antenna exit site 22

Figure 12. Schematic showing the correct and incorrect orientation of the tip of the needle against the body wall when the shielded needle technique is used to create an antenna exit site. 23

Figure 13. Two simple interrupted sutures 24

Conversion Factors

SI to Inch/Pound

Multiply	By		To obtain
		Length	
centimeter (cm)	0.3937		inch (in.)
millimeter (mm)	0.03937		inch (in.)
		Volume	
liter (L)	33.82		ounce, fluid (fl. oz)
liter (L)	2.113		pint (pt)
liter (L)	1.057		quart (qt)
liter (L)	0.2642		gallon (gal)
liter (L)	61.02		cubic inch (in^3)
		Mass	
gram (g)	0.03527		ounce, avoirdupois (oz)

Temperature in degrees Celsius (°C) may be converted to degrees Fahrenheit (°F) as follows: °F=(1.8×°C)+32.

Concentrations of chemical constituents in water are given either in milligrams per liter (mg/L) or micrograms per liter (µg/L).

A Standard Operating Procedure for the Surgical Implantation of Transmitters in Juvenile Salmonids

By T.L. Liedtke, J.W. Beeman, and L.P. Gee

Introduction

Biotelemetry is a useful tool to monitor the movements of animals and is widely applied in fisheries research. Radio or acoustic technology can be used, depending on the study design and the environmental conditions in the study area. A broad definition of telemetry also includes the use of Passive Integrated Transponder (PIT) tags, either separately or with a radio or acoustic transmitter. To use telemetry, fish must be equipped with a transmitter. Although there are several attachment procedures available, surgical implantation of transmitters in the abdominal cavity is recognized as the best technique for long-term telemetry studies in general (Stasko and Pincock, 1977; Winter, 1996; Jepsen, 2003), and specifically for juvenile salmonids, *Oncorhynchus spp.* (Adams and others, 1998a, 1998b; Martinelli and others, 1998; Hall and others, 2009). Studies that use telemetry assume that the processes by which the animals are captured, handled, and tagged, as well as the act of carrying the transmitter, will have minimal effect on their behavior and performance. This assumption, commonly stated as a lack of transmitter effects, must be valid if telemetry studies are to describe accurately the movements and behavior of an entire population of interest, rather than the subset of that population that carries transmitters.

This document describes a standard operating procedure (SOP) for surgical implantation of radio or acoustic transmitters in juvenile salmonids. The procedures were developed from a broad base of published information, laboratory experiments, and practical experience in tagging thousands of fish for numerous studies of juvenile salmon movements near Columbia River and Snake River hydroelectric dams. Staff from the Western Fisheries Research Center's Columbia River Research Laboratory (CRRL) frequently have used telemetry studies to evaluate new structures or operations at hydroelectric dams in the Columbia River Basin, and these evaluations typically require large numbers of tagged fish. For example, a study conducted at the dams on the Columbia River and funded by the U.S. Army Corps of Engineers required tagging and monitoring of 40,000 juvenile salmon during a 3-month migration period (Counihan and others, 2006a, 2006b; Perry and others, 2006). To meet the demands of such a large study, the authors and CRRL staff refined the SOP to increase efficiency in the tagging process while maintaining high standards of fish care. The SOP has been used in laboratory and field settings for more than 15 years, and consistently has produced low mortality rates (<1 percent) and transmitter loss rates (<0.01 percent) in the 24–36 hours after tagging.

In addition to describing the detailed surgical procedures required for transmitter implantation, this document provides guidance on fish collection, handling and holding, and the release of tagged fish. Although often overlooked, or at least underemphasized, these processes can have a large impact on the outcome of the tagging procedure. Stress associated with the individual steps in handling and tagging can be cumulative and lethal (Maule and others, 1988; Wedemeyer and others, 1990; Portz and others, 2006), so the goal is to provide the best possible fish care at every step in order to manage the overall effect on study fish.

Purpose and Applicability

The purpose of this document is to provide guidelines and procedures for the surgical implantation of radio or acoustic transmitters into juvenile salmonids. Guidelines for fish collection, handling, holding, and release are included to reduce stressors to fish and to increase the likelihood of a positive surgical outcome. The clear, specific guidance in the SOP, when monitored and enforced, keeps the application of procedures consistent across studies, personnel, and time, and increases opportunity for comparisons across telemetry studies using similar procedures.

The SOP can be applied in studies that surgically implant radio or acoustic transmitters in the body cavity of juvenile salmonids of both natural and hatchery origin. Radio and acoustic transmitters require slightly different implantation procedures because radio transmitters commonly have an external antenna, whereas acoustic transmitters do not have an external antenna. The SOP also can be used for the surgical implantation of PIT tags, either separately or with a radio or acoustic transmitter.

Although the procedures were developed and refined in the Columbia River Basin for large-scale telemetry studies, the guiding principles behind the procedures can be applied readily to other studies and locations. The SOP has been adapted for work in the Sacramento and San Joaquin Rivers in California (San Joaquin River Group Authority, 2008, 2009; California Department of Water Resources, 2012) and in the marine waters of Puget Sound, Washington. Although the SOP is intended to guide the surgical implantation of transmitters in juvenile salmon, it can be modified and expanded to provide guidance for other species or life stages. Many elements of the procedures generally are applicable to the handling and tagging of all fish.

Guiding Principles

Several guiding principles should be applied to studies using telemetry to minimize transmitter and handling effects. Entities that use telemetry invest considerable amounts of money into monitoring equipment, transmitters, surgical equipment, and staff time in order to address their research questions. Each individual tagged fish is a significant investment; therefore, efforts should be made to ensure that the potential for handling and transmitter effects are controlled, and that tagged fish can reliably represent the untagged population.

Develop Surgical Proficiency

Personnel performing any transmitter attachment procedure (hereafter referred to as taggers) must be proficient in order to minimize stress to fish (Cooke and others, 2003; Wagner and Cooke, 2005). Surgical implantation generally is more challenging than other attachment methods (that is, external or gastric), and requires a level of manual dexterity that may not be possessed by all taggers. Practice sessions are essential to positive tagging outcomes (Smith and others, 2009), and ideally, taggers will practice on fish of the same species, size, and life stage that will be used for the study. The use of surrogates may be required when the study fish are threatened, endangered, or otherwise difficult to obtain. Surrogates should provide the best possible match to the target species and size. In cases where proficient taggers have been inactive for a period, or when a new species or size class is being studied, taggers should participate in a refresher session to reinforce proper technique.

A tagger training program should include a knowledgeable mentor, the opportunity to practice on model systems, and a continuous evaluation and feedback loop. New taggers must have access to a proficient mentor with broad knowledge of fish handling and tagging procedures. Many veterinarians have specialized training in fish medicine, making consultation and collaboration powerful approaches to developing or refining transmitter implantation techniques (Wagner and Cooke, 2005; Harms and

Lewbart, 2011). The use of model systems, rather than live fish, can be helpful during the initial tagging practice sessions. For example, when learning suturing techniques, taggers can practice on bananas, orange peels, or artificial skin until surgical knots are tied correctly and consistently. Once proficient with the model system, taggers can advance to a more realistic surrogate, such as dead fish, where they can refine their skills without attention to fish handling. Once they have mastered basic tagging skills, trainees can advance to practice on live fish and the corresponding fish-handling requirements.

Mentors should evaluate proficiency and provide feedback to taggers throughout the training program. Tagging proficiency can be evaluated by holding practice fish in tanks and monitoring short-term (days to weeks) survival, transmitter loss, and the external and internal condition of the fish. Necropsies should be conducted post-tagging, with both the tagger and the mentor present to visualize transmitter position within the body cavity, incision apposition, and any potential effects on internal organs. Photographs of practice fish can help document proficiency, and video recordings can be useful in documenting tagging methods and as a learning tool for future trainees. Another measure of tagging proficiency that is easily quantifiable and linked with the stress response of fish is the length of time needed to complete a surgical procedure. Taggers should strive to become competent and efficient in order to limit fish exposure to anesthesia and handling. Speed, however, should not compromise proper execution of the procedure. The time required to complete a surgery should be monitored, and the time required by a trainee can be compared to the time required by an experienced tagger as one indicator of proficiency.

Many resources are available to researchers who want to develop surgical proficiency. Surgery text books (for example, Slatter, 2003) should be reviewed for the principles underlying suture material and surgical knots. We recommend that researchers consult an experienced veterinarian or medical professional for specific instruction in surgical knot-tying techniques. Additionally, numerous medical videos are available on the Internet that illustrate basic surgical knots.

Anticipate and Manage Tagger Effects

When multiple taggers are used, the experimental design should anticipate some level of "tagger effects," with potentially different outcomes for individual taggers. Even with experienced and proficient taggers, there are likely to be some minor, short-term differences, although these are often difficult to assess. The probability that fish tagged by different taggers will have different short-term mortality rates (the easiest response to measure) is low, but mortality is only a crude indicator of tagging success (Mulcahy, 2003; Jepsen and others, 2008). Differences in stress response or wound healing among fish tagged by different taggers are more likely to occur, but are more difficult to detect. For example, response differences may arise from fish being held out of water for varying lengths of time because of differences in surgical procedure time.

Anticipating tagger effects is the best approach to managing them. The most simplistic approach is to use a single, experienced tagger throughout the study. If a single tagger is not sufficient, minimize the number of taggers and train them all using the same SOP and training program. When multiple taggers are used, the schedule should be configured so each tagger contributes equally to all study treatment groups. Researchers should be prepared to quantitatively assess tagger effects by formally evaluating response metrics by tagger (for example, see Beeman and others, 2011).

Reduce and Refine Fish Handling

Researchers should use the utmost care when handling fish before, during, and after the surgical procedure to minimize the stress to fish and to control the risk of infection. Stress due to handling may reduce survival and the capacity to handle additional stressors such as tagging (Kelsh and Shields, 1996). Fish will be more vulnerable to infection as a result of any handling procedure that interrupts the outer mucus layer (Harms, 2005), including contact with nets, measuring, weighing, and transmitter implantation. The tagging operation should be designed to limit fish handling, and especially fish transfers, to control these risks. Study fish should be collected using the least destructive and least stressful method that is effective. Holding containers should have dark interiors and covers to minimize disturbance and fish loss due to jumping (Portz and others, 2006), and should be monitored to maintain appropriate water-quality. Dissolved oxygen (DO) concentrations should be maintained near saturation, and water temperature should be maintained within a few degrees of the water where the fish were collected and will be released (Kelsh and Shields, 1996). Differences in water temperature larger than several degrees Celsius (°C) can be managed by mixing the source and destination water to produce a gradual temperature change (Stickney and Kohler, 1990; Kelsh and Shields, 1996). Researchers should use extreme caution when handling and tagging juvenile salmonids at high water temperatures (about 18–20°C).

Tagging operations should be designed to reduce the number of fish transfers in an effort to control the stress to study fish. Typically several transfers are involved as fish are moved from the pre-tagging location, through the anesthesia process, into a post-tagging holding location, and finally to the release location. Working within the logistical constraints for the study and the tagging location, researchers should establish the fish movement path with the fewest transfers. For example, the source of fish to be tagged should be near the tagging operation so that fish can be netted directly into anesthesia. As fish are tagged, they can be placed in a portable holding container, such as a bucket, that can then be transported to the release location without an additional transfer.

Standard handling techniques should be refined to reduce stress to fish and to avoid damage to the mucus layer. Where possible, use a crowding device to aggregate fish gently in a container prior to removal rather than pursuing them aggressively with a net. Such devices can be quickly fabricated from plastic pipe and mesh fabric or more rigid netting. Reducing the water level in the container is another approach to crowding. We recommend use of a sanctuary net, which is designed to transfer fish in water, rather than removing them from water in a standard net. The use of water-to-water transfers has been shown to reduce handling stress (Matthews and others, 1986; Flagg and Harrell, 1990). Although sanctuary nets can be difficult to purchase in appropriate sizes for juvenile salmonids, they are relatively easy to fabricate using standard nets and water-resistant fabric.

Practice Aseptic Techniques

When surgeries are performed on animals in a veterinary hospital, the goal of aseptic technique is to create a surgical environment that is completely sterile. This level of asepsis is difficult to achieve in field settings, and the aquatic environment poses additional challenges to keeping the equipment, incision site, and transmitter free of contamination. Even in controlled laboratory settings, strictly sterile procedures cannot be accomplished on fish (American Fisheries Society, 2004; Harms, 2005). Despite these challenges, steps should be taken to reduce the risk of infection when invasive procedures such as surgery are performed on fish.

Medical-grade exam gloves should be worn by the tagger and any personnel handling fish, instruments, or transmitters. The primary function of gloves is to reduce the transmission of potential pathogens from fish to fish, but they also protect the tagger from anesthetics, disinfectants, and potential waterborne pathogens. Ideally, sterile gloves would be used and changed between fish; however, it is virtually impossible to avoid contamination from either the fish or the water source during a procedure. At a minimum, clean gloves should be worn and gloves should be changed regularly.

Equipment, such as tanks, containers, nets, air stones, and the tagging platform, should be disinfected between successive tagging sessions. A thorough drying period is a useful addition to chemical disinfection for equipment (Harms, 2005). Because the water source is the route of pathogen exchange, the environment should be kept as clean and dry as possible during a given tagging session.

Irrigation of the gills during surgery presents a risk of contamination of the peritoneal cavity. The water used for irrigation likely is pathogen-rich, so steps must be taken to prevent this water from contaminating the incision area or entering the body cavity (Harms, 2005). This need can be met using a tagging platform that holds fish in a reclined position so that the incision is higher than the head. Taggers must monitor the irrigation system to ensure that water does not overflow the gills and enter the body cavity through the incision.

Surgical instruments should be sterilized prior to each individual procedure to reduce infection and tissue reaction (Marty and Summerfelt, 1986; Moore and others, 1990; Mulcahy, 2003; Harms, 2005). Small autoclaves or pressure cookers can be used for this purpose. When tagging large numbers of fish in a field setting, there may not be enough instruments available to allow for prior sterilization and packaging of instruments for each procedure. Under these circumstances, instruments should initially be sterile and then should be disinfected and rinsed between procedures (Lucas, 1989; Lacroix and others, 2004). This SOP requires that chlorhexidine diacetate (hereafter referred to as chlorhexidine) be used to disinfect instruments between procedures, and several sets of instruments are used in rotation to ensure sufficient contact time (10 minutes) for full efficacy. If instruments are not rotated, sequential procedures must be separated by enough time to allow for the full contact time in the disinfectant. Following disinfection, instruments must be rinsed well with distilled or deionized water to remove potentially toxic chemical residue. Instrument sterilization or disinfection procedures must be strictly enforced because fish-to-fish transmission of pathogens has been documented (Elliott and Pascho, 2001).

The transmitter deserves special care in regard to aseptic technique because it will remain in contact with the tissues of the fish for extended periods. Ideally, transmitters would be sterilized prior to implantation, but this expectation is difficult to meet because the most common sterilization technique uses heat, which can damage transmitter components. Alternative approaches, such as gas and chemical sterilization, are available, but typically are limited to controlled laboratory settings because of their potentially hazardous nature. A veterinary or medical office may be able to pre-sterilize transmitters and package them for transport into the field (Mulcahy, 2003). A common approach is to disinfect transmitters using the procedures established for disinfecting instruments. Extra care should be taken to ensure adequate contact time with the disinfectant and thorough rinsing of residues from the transmitter. Researchers also should ensure that the disinfectant will not damage the transmitter coating. After transmitters have been disinfected or sterilized, they should be handled only with clean instruments or gloved hands, avoiding contact with any source water or potentially contaminated surfaces until they are implanted.

Manage Anesthesia

Tricaine methanesulfonate (MS-222®), also known as Finquel®, is the only chemical anesthetic approved by the U.S. Food and Drug Administration for use in fish at the time of this writing (2012). Ideally, anesthetics should have a rapid induction time (about 3 minutes), a short recovery time (<5 minutes), and no persistent effects on fish physiology, allowing for immediate release of fish (Marking and Meyer, 1985; Summerfelt and Smith, 1990). MS-222® does not meet the definition of an ideal anesthetic because it requires a 21-day withdrawal period for fish that may be captured and used as food (Schnick, 2006). Fisheries researchers clearly need additional options in the choice of anesthetics, and efforts are underway to evaluate several candidate chemicals. MS-222® was selected for use in this SOP because of its proven efficacy, and the 21-day withdrawal period is not limiting since humans are not likely to consume juvenile salmon.

Because of the hazardous nature of MS-222®, the stock solution should be prepared in a laboratory setting, following the guidance on the package label and the material safety data sheet. Stock solutions should be kept in amber bottles because the material will degrade in sunlight. To ensure full efficacy, avoid exposing the solution to high temperatures and regularly replace the stock solution.

The effectiveness of MS-222® as an anesthetic varies with working concentration, water temperature, species, and individual fish response. Adjustments to the anesthesia concentration should be made based on fish response and water conditions at the tagging location. The depth of anesthesia can be recognized by monitoring a series of physiological changes, beginning with a loss of reactivity to stimuli (stage 1), and progressing to a total loss of equilibrium (stage 4), loss of all reflex activity (stage 5), and eventual medullary collapse (stage 6) (Summerfelt and Smith, 1990). Surgical implantation procedures require stages 4–5 anesthesia and regular monitoring of the ventilation rate to prevent respiratory failure (stage 6). The concentration of the anesthesia should not be any higher than needed to achieve an induction time of about 3 minutes because the risk of mortality is inversely related to induction time (Summerfelt and Smith, 1990). Total exposure time also is an important consideration because prolonged exposure can lead to mortality (Mulford, 1984; Summerfelt and Smith, 1990).

A stock solution of 100 mg of MS-222®/mL water has a pH of about 2 in deionized water (Summerfelt and Smith, 1990), but may be less acidic in other water sources, depending on their buffering capacity. To counteract the low pH and to minimize the corresponding physiological effects on fish, the addition of sodium bicarbonate is recommended to buffer the anesthetic solution to a pH of about 7 (Wedemeyer, 1970; Soivio and others, 1977; Harms, 2005). Separate stock solutions should be prepared for MS-222® and sodium bicarbonate because they form a white, oily precipitate when they are mixed at high concentrations.

Exposure to MS-222® induces immediate physiological changes (Wedemeyer, 1970; Houston and others, 1971; Strange and Schreck, 1978), some of which can be long-lasting (Soivio and others, 1977). A state of asphyxia develops because of reductions in the heart rate and gill ventilation rate, and is compounded by swelling of erythrocytes, which further restricts circulation (Soivio and others, 1977). The oxygen debt that is incurred during exposure to anesthesia must be overcome during the recovery period. To facilitate recovery, fish should be placed in water with a high DO concentration immediately following the surgical procedure.

To maintain effective and consistent anesthesia throughout a tagging session, the anesthesia bath must be replaced regularly. In a typical field setting, a single anesthesia container is used to anesthetize a number of fish. Each fish added to the container removes part of the oxygen and anesthetic and adds mucus, carbon dioxide, and ammonia to the solution. The transfer of fish to the container typically also involves the addition of at least nominal amounts of water, diluting the working concentration of the anesthetic. Water temperature in the isolated anesthesia container typically will increase with time, influencing fish response. Regularly changing the anesthesia bath will minimize these variables and ensure consistent application.

Construct an Effective Tagging Station

A tagging station should include a tagging platform to hold fish with the ventral surface exposed and some space to allow easy access to equipment and supplies (for example, transmitters and instruments). Plastic, closed cell foam, or other materials that do not absorb significant amounts of water should be used in the construction of the tagging station so that it can be effectively disinfected. Any surfaces that will directly contact fish should be smooth and kept moist to prevent damage to the skin, scales, or mucus layer of the fish. Similarly, surfaces designed to hold equipment and supplies should be kept dry to prevent exposure to any waterborne pathogens in the water source. Designing the station to hold the fish in a reclined position, with the head at the lowest point, allows for good irrigation while controlling the risk of irrigation water entering the body cavity through the incision. Good lighting is another consideration. Adjusting the height of the tagging surface so that the tagger is positioned comfortably will improve the efficiency of the tagging process. Example tagging platforms include an acrylic glass (or PLEXIGLAS®) frame (fig. 1) or a block of closed-cell foam modified to hold a fish (fig. 2).

Figure 1. An example surgical platform constructed of acrylic glass.

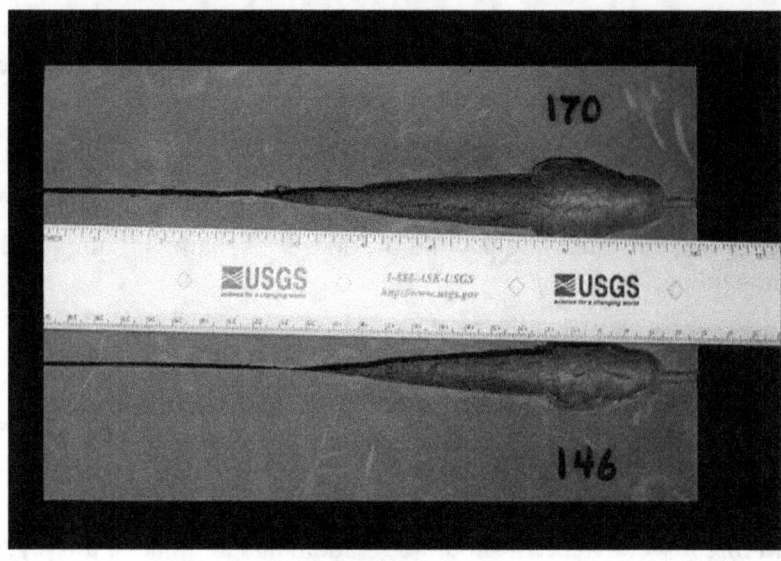

Figure 2. An example surgical platform consisting of closed-cell foam with sections carved to support the fish in proper surgical orientation.

Fish must have their gills irrigated during the surgery, so the tagging station must accommodate either gravity-feed irrigation or a pump system. This SOP recommends the use of a gravity feed irrigation system due to its ease of operation (no power is needed) and high reliability (fig. 3). The irrigation system includes two water containers (buckets or carboys): one labeled "sedation" that delivers a light dose of anesthetic, and one that delivers fresh water. The containers are positioned side-by-side on an elevated platform or shelf over the tagging platform. The containers should be about 45–60 cm above the tagging platform to provide adequate flow. Each container has tubing that links the container to a junction connector, which joins the two tubing lines (fig. 3). Following the junction, there is a single line of tubing that enters the fish's mouth to provide irrigation. Each container has a valve that allows the tagger to control the rate of flow through the tubing. This system allows the tagger to provide fish with sedation water, fresh water, or a combination of sedation and fresh water. An example tagging station, including the gravity feed irrigation system, is shown in figure 4.

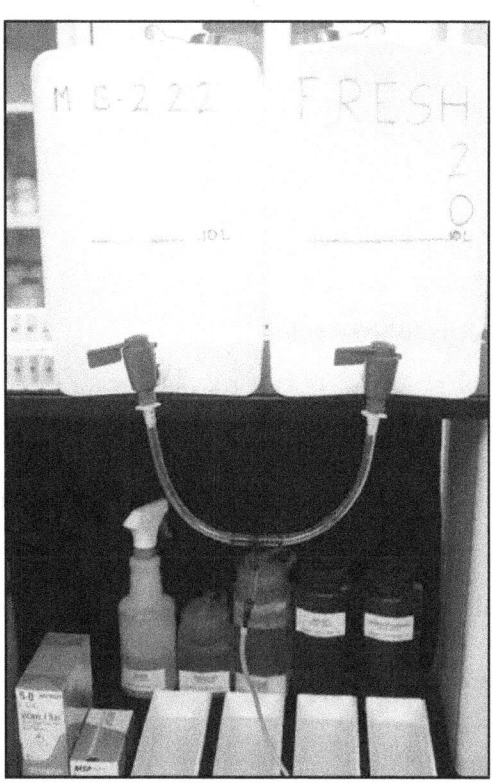

Figure 3.   An example gravity feed irrigation system. One container holds fresh water and one container holds a light dose (sedation) of MS-222®. Both containers have valves to control flow. The tubing from each container is joined, and a single line of tubing continues to the surgery platform.

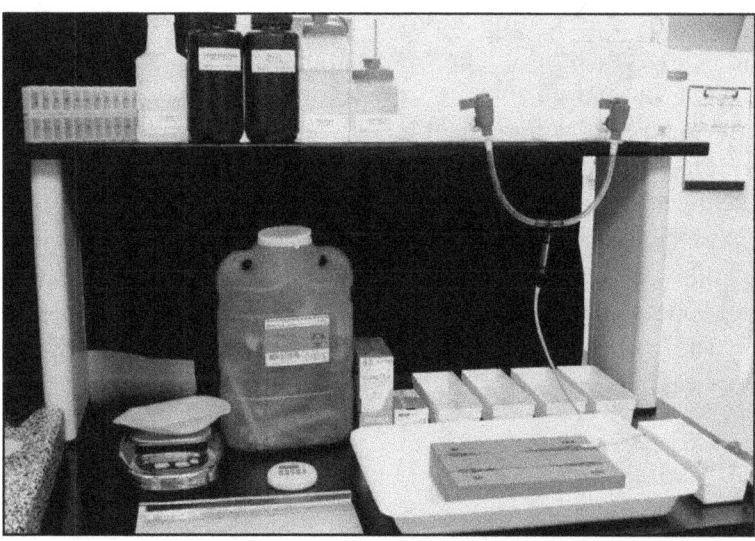

Figure 4.   An example tagging station with gravity feed irrigation system, instrument disinfection and rinse trays, and surgical platform.

Procedures

Because of the tight linkages between fish handling and surgical outcome, the SOP outlines procedures prior to and following the implantation of the transmitter. The procedures begin with fish collection and continue until tagged fish are released for monitoring. Although procedures may vary somewhat between individual studies, based on study design and logistics, the general workflow should be similar. Workflow steps generally include: (1) fish collection or acquisition, (2) possible transport to the tagging location, (3) a holding period before tagging (pre-tag holding), (4) an anesthesia process, (5) morphometric data collection and review of fish condition, (6) implantation of the transmitter, (7) short-term recovery, (8) a holding period following tagging (post-tag holding), (9) possible transport to a release location, and (10) release of tagged fish for monitoring. For the purposes of this SOP, 19-L buckets are used to hold fish, beginning with the anesthesia process and continuing at least through short-term recovery, and most commonly through the release of tagged fish.

To aid in study planning, a detailed list of suggested materials is provided in appendix A. Abbreviated, step-by-step procedures are provided in appendix B. The narrative procedures below provide rationale and background for the critical SOP steps to allow the researcher to understand the principles behind the procedures.

Fish Collection, Holding, and Transport

Collection: Study fish should be collected using the least destructive and least stressful method that is effective. Seining, trapping, or other collection techniques may be used or fish can be obtained directly from a rearing facility, such as a hatchery or research laboratory. Dams or other barriers often have fish collection facilities that can provide access to fish for studies. When selecting a collection method, consider any biases inherent in the technique. For example, a given trapping method might be biased toward catching primarily small fish, which will have the effect of restricting the size range of the fish that will be tagged and monitored. Fish that obviously are injured, diseased, or excessively burdened by parasites should not be retained for tagging. If fish are collected by a group other than the group performing the surgeries, coordination of the fish-handling details will be critical. Groups should agree on the most appropriate handling processes and perhaps generate an SOP to ensure consistent procedures throughout the study.

Holding periods: Following collection or acquisition, fish should be held for 12–36 hours (ideally 24 hours) prior to tagging. The pre-tag holding period for a group of fish begins once fish are in the care of the researcher and ends when surgical procedures begin. If fish must be transported from the collection location to the tagging location, the pre-tag holding time begins when fish arrive at the tagging location. Following tagging, fish should be held 18–36 hours (optimally about 24 hours). The post-tag holding period begins when the last fish for a given tagging session is placed in the post-tag holding container. The holding period ends when fish are removed from the post-tag holding container in preparation for release.

The rationale for pre-tag and post-tag holding is to allow fish to recover from acute stressors, such as collection, transport, and tagging (Stickney and Kohler, 1990; Kelsh and Shields, 1996). A combination of stressors (for example, collection and tagging) can be lethal even if fish can tolerate them independently (Portz and others, 2006), so the stressors should be separated in time (Stickney and Kohler, 1990). Although the duration and severity of the stressor can produce significant variability in stress responses, such as plasma cortisol (Pickering and others, 1982), levels frequently return to baseline conditions within about 24 hours following an acute stressor, such as handling (Strange and Schreck, 1978; Jepsen and others, 2001). An additional rationale for the pre-tag holding period is to restrict access to food so that fish enter a post-absorptive state prior to the invasive procedure (Summerfelt and Smith, 1990).

Although there are compelling reasons to hold fish both before and after tagging, these reasons must be balanced against the risk of additional stress to fish, particularly fish in migratory life stages, such as juvenile salmonids. Actively migrating juvenile salmonids may incur high mortality when held for extended periods, even without the stress of a surgical procedure. The pre-tag and post-tag holding periods must be considered in light of the entire duration of holding, including the time needed to complete the tagging. The total amount of time that juvenile salmon are held captive should be limited to about 48 hours. The recommended holding periods are defined as ranges so that adjustments can be made based on individual study objectives or logistical constraints, while accommodating an overall limited holding period of about 48 hours.

Holding conditions: Fish should be held at low stocking densities in dark containers with lids. Container lids reduce visual disturbances, such as bright sunlight or passing shadows, and reduce the risk of fish loss from jumping. If multiple species of fish are collected, hold the species in separate but comparable containers. This separation is especially important when there are large size differences between the species that could induce a stress response in the smaller fish. Pre-tag holding densities should not exceed 20 g of fish per L of water, and post-tag holding densities should not exceed 10 g of fish per L of water (see appendix B for formula to calculate holding density). The recommended pre-tag and post-tag holding densities are conservative relative to standard hatchery transportation practices for salmonids, which vary but range from 60 to 240 g/L (Piper and others, 1982). The post-tag density is more restrictive than the pre-tag density for several reasons. First, there is commonly a need to transport untagged fish, and the recommended pre-tag density allows some flexibility in transport options while controlling crowding stress. Second, the tagged fish reflect a significant financial and time investment, and will be the basis of the planned study, so a conservative approach is warranted to minimize potential crowding stress post-tagging.

Pre-tag and post-tag holding conditions should be configured to minimize fish transfers and to facilitate the release of tagged fish. An approach we commonly use to meet this challenge is to hold fish in small, portable containers so that the container can be moved as needed without direct handling of the fish. The small containers can be immersed in a larger container to maintain water-quality if water exchange is established between the containers and the tank (fig. 5). At the start of the tagging procedure, a transfer can be avoided if the holding of untagged fish is well designed. Specifically, untagged fish should be held close to the tagging location (or in a small tank or cooler that can be carried or moved on a dolly system to the tagging location), rather than holding fish in a distant, stationary container and then netting small groups of fish into a container closer to the tagging location for ease of processing. If large numbers of fish need to be held, add additional small containers rather than move to a larger container so that portability is maintained. Alternately, the anesthesia container can be carried from the distant holding tank to the tagging location.

Figure 5. Holding tank with immersed 19-liter perforated recovery containers. The perforations allow water exchange between the containers and the larger volume of the tank.

At the end of the tagging procedure, fish ideally would be held in small containers that can be used for recovery, post-tag holding, transport (if needed), and release. At a minimum, the post-tag holding should be configured so that tagged fish can be released without a net transfer. When there are limited options for releasing tagged fish, use water-to-water transfer techniques such as pouring fish out of a container or moving them through a pipe.

In addition to the general holding recommendations outlined above, both pre- and post-tag holding have specialized requirements: pre-tag fish should be monitored for behavior and condition, and post-tag fish must have access to air. Monitor untagged fish for significant scale loss, wounds, or atypical behavior, such as compromised swimming ability that may result from stress or injury from collection or transport. The discovery of moribund or dead fish during the pre-tag holding period is an ominous sign and likely will lead to increased post-tagging mortality. Following tagging, and throughout the post-tag holding period and any needed transport, salmonids (physostomes) need access to the air-water interface in order to regain neutral buoyancy. Attachment of the transmitter to fish induces negative buoyancy, which could cause altered depth distribution (resting on the bottom) or increased metabolic requirements due to increased fin use or faster swimming (Gallepp and Magnuson, 1972). Juvenile salmon can counteract the weight of the transmitter relatively quickly by gulping air and increasing the volume of the swim bladder, provided they have access to air. Fried and others (1976) reported that tagged Atlantic salmon smolts (*Salmo salar*) denied access to air after tagging were unable to regain neutral buoyancy, even after 24 hours. Alternately, tagged fish provided access to the air-water interface were able to adjust their buoyancy within 6 hours (Fried and others, 1976). Handling can cause fish to expel air, which changes their buoyancy (Harvey and others, 1968), so gentle handling in all aspects of fish collection and tagging should be emphasized.

Water-quality during holding: Water-quality must be monitored and maintained in all containers used to hold fish. Water temperature, DO, and total dissolved gas (TDG) are the water-quality parameters that need to be maintained within the limits defined by the SOP. Ideally, fish would be held using the water where they were collected or into which they will be released. When the water source does not offer appropriate water-quality, the holding system must have the capacity to adjust to meet the minimum SOP standards. If, during monitoring, a water-quality parameter is outside of the defined limits, action must be taken to bring the parameter into compliance with the SOP. A proactive monitoring approach generally will detect water-quality deviations before they become severe, and then they are more quickly remedied.

Water temperature is a critical consideration for tagging operations because of the risk of thermal stress. Fish should not be transferred between water sources until the difference in water temperature between the water sources is less than or equal to 2°C. Changes in water temperature exceeding 2°C require tempering to prevent thermal stress (Stickney and Kohler, 1990; Kelsch and Shields, 1996). Tempering is the process of mixing water sources to reach an intermediate temperature. Therefore, prior to exposing fish to a new water source, the temperature of the current water source and the new water source must be measured. If the temperature difference is less than or equal to 2°C, the transfer can be made without tempering. If the temperature difference is greater than 2°C, then water in the container holding fish should be tempered at a rate of 0.5°C per 15 minutes until the temperature difference between the two water sources is less than or equal to 2°C. New source water should be added in small amounts multiple times over 15 minutes to gradually change the temperature. Once the temperature difference between the two water sources is less than or equal to 2°C, fish can be transferred to the new water source. The same instrument should be used to measure both water sources to ensure accurate measurement of the temperature differential.

The DO concentration in all holding containers must be 80–130 percent saturation. Supplemental oxygen or aeration can be used, in combination with air diffusers, to supplement the DO in source water, as needed. We caution that supplemental systems are prone to supersaturating the water, so they must be carefully regulated. There is one exception to these DO saturation standards, and it will be addressed in the post-tagging recovery procedures.

Total dissolved gas should be monitored when it has the potential to be an issue, and should not exceed 110 percent saturation in water sources that contain fish. Water passed over high-head spillways can entrain gas and create dissolved gas supersaturation in the water. Exposure to TDG can be an acute or chronic source of stress, and can lead to gas bubble trauma (Mesa and others, 2000). Control of TDG levels typically is done with a degassing column where source water cascades over a collection of high-surface-area objects (for example, plastic rings) so that gas is released. Following passage through the degassing column, water has reduced TDG levels and can be supplied to holding containers.

Water-quality in small containers that lack exchange with a larger volume can quickly become compromised. Many such small containers are used during tagging procedures, including anesthesia and recovery containers. Taggers and support staff must be vigilant in monitoring water-quality and refreshing containers regularly to maintain SOP standards.

Fish transport: Study fish may need to be transported before tagging, after tagging, or both, depending on the study design and site logistics. Untagged fish might need to be moved from the collection point to the tagging location, and tagged fish might require transport from the tagging location to the point of release. Transport operations should be designed to minimize stress to fish and to maintain the water-quality parameters outlined in the SOP. Select a route of travel for the shortest and smoothest ride to minimize jarring. If water temperature rises significantly during transport, cooling actions, such as the addition of ice, may be required. Researchers should be aware that most commercially produced ice contains chlorine, which can be harmful to fish. We recommend freezing source water in small containers or double-bagging commercial ice to prevent the exchange of melted ice water with the source water.

Fish Size Criteria

The size of fish suitable for tagging depends on the size of the transmitter used. The smallest transmitter that will meet study objectives should be used because larger transmitters (in similar size fish) are more likely to induce transmitter effects. An estimate that can be used to evaluate the risk of transmitter effects is the transmitter-to-body weight ratio (or tag burden). The tag burden should be calculated using the combined mass of all transmitters or tags implanted. For example, in some cases, a PIT tag is implanted in combination with a radio or acoustic transmitter, and the tag burden should include the weight of both tags. The most commonly accepted limit for tag burden is from Winter (1996), who recommends that transmitter weight in air does not exceed 2 percent of fish body weight in air. Transmitter effects correlated with high tag burdens include increased mortality and transmitter expulsion (Moore and others, 1990; Lacroix and others, 2004; Jepsen and others, 2008; Hall and others, 2009), reduced growth (Jepsen and others, 2008), and reduced swimming performance (Adams and others, 1998b; Zale and others, 2005).

Transmitter sizes have been reduced through technological advances, but even small transmitters, in small fish, can exceed the 2-percent tag burden rule of thumb. In our experience, the performance of juvenile salmonids is not significantly compromised when tag burdens of up to 5 percent are used (Adams and others 1998a, 1998b; Martinelli and others, 1998; Perry and others, 2001). When the tag burden exceeds 5 percent, the transmitter effects are variable, and may occur more frequently (Hall and others 2009; Brown and others, 2010). Considering the consequences of an excessive tag burden, we have set a maximum acceptable tag burden limit of 5 percent for this SOP; smaller tag burdens are preferable.

In addition to tag burden, other considerations may influence the fish size criteria established, including transmitter volume, length, diameter, shape, density, and coating, any of which also may influence fish behavior and performance (Sakaris and others, 2005; Penne and others, 2007).

Tagging Preparations

Transmitters: Transmitters should be prepared for implantation by confirming their operation and disinfecting them. The transmitter characteristics (that is, frequency, pulse rate, and so on) should be confirmed to be as specified, as errors can occur when transmitters are labeled or packaged. A pre-tag water exposure trial can be useful in evaluating whether water intrusion into transmitters might cause failure. If PIT tags are used, their function also should be confirmed before tagging. Although PIT tags do not carry a battery, they can still fail to function when energized. If transmitters were not sterilized and pre-packaged for use during a tagging session, they must be disinfected before they are implanted. Transmitters should be immersed in chlorhexidine disinfectant solution for a minimum of 15 minutes. The disinfectant exposure time for transmitters is somewhat longer than instruments (15 minutes versus 10 minutes) to ensure efficacy because transmitters stay in close contact with tissue for extended time periods. Following disinfection, transmitters should be rinsed well with distilled or deionized water, and rinsing should continue until there are no signs of suds or residue. Once the transmitters have been disinfected, they must not be handled by anything other than clean instruments or clean, gloved hands.

Tag station and supplies: Prepare the tag station and tagging supplies. Set up the irrigation system (gravity feed or pump) by filling containers from the pre-tag holding or post-tag holding water source. Do not fill containers until the near the time of tagging to prevent the water temperature from fluctuating. A scale, weigh boat, and measuring board will be needed for tagging, and they should be clean at the start of the tagging session. Scales should be calibrated weekly to ensure accuracy. The measuring board should be made of smooth material and be in good condition to avoid damage to the skin or scales of the fish. As further protection against skin damage, we placed 1–2 mL of a diluted mucous restorative solution on the weigh boat and the measuring board. We typically have used a mucous restorative product, Stress Coat® (manufactured by Aquarium Pharmaceuticals Inc.), but there are many similar products on the market and any of them will be effective in protecting fish (the SOP will continue to reference Stress Coat® for clarity). Working surfaces will need to be coated regularly with Stress Coat® throughout the tagging session to keep the working surfaces wet. Expendable tagging supplies (suture packets, gloves, and solutions) should be positioned near the tagging platform, on a dry surface, to prevent contamination.

Instruments: Surgical instruments should be organized into sets and arranged in individual disinfection trays. Each tagging session should begin with sterile surgical instruments. The standard procedure for instrument sterilization is to wrap instruments in a cloth and to secure them with autoclave tape, which is designed to indicate exposure to sterilization temperatures. At the start of a tagging session, the instrument packet should be examined to confirm that the autoclave tape has changed color (confirming exposure to the appropriate temperature), the packet should be unwrapped, and instruments should be sorted into sets. A complete set of instruments includes a needle driver, a microscalpel holder, and forceps (see appendix A for detailed descriptions of the instruments). Each instrument set should be placed into a separate disinfection container with chlorhexidine disinfectant solution. At least one rinse container, filled with distilled or deionized water also will be needed.

We recommend the use of micro scalpel blades rather than standard scalpel blades because of the thin body wall of juvenile salmonids and the risk of damage to organs when making the incision. Additionally, the micro scalpel blades can improve tagger confidence and, therefore, can improve tagging speed and efficiency. The blades can be purchased in a wide variety of blade angles and lengths, and the appropriate blade should be selected through experimentation and practice. Our preference is to use two lengths of micro scalpel with a 15-degree blade angle: a 3-mm blade for thin-bodied fish such as Chinook, sockeye, and coho, and a 5-mm blade for steelhead or other fish with a relatively thicker body wall. Micro scalpels are disposable and can be purchased as a complete unit (a full blade and handle) or as a stand-alone blade. The stand-alone blades are less expensive than the full scalpels, and are designed to be attached to a reusable stainless steel micro scalpel handle (fig. 6). Narratives in this SOP assume that micro scalpel holders will be used.

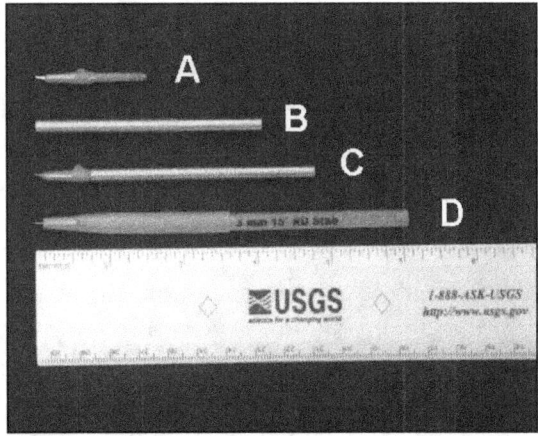

Figure 6. Example micro scalpel configurations. A disposable micro scalpel blade with a threaded end (A) can be combined with a stainless steel handle (B) to make a complete scalpel (C). A fully disposable micro scalpel (D) is an alternate configuration.

Surgical instrument sets will be rotated throughout the tagging session to ensure 10 minutes of exposure time in chlorhexidine. Depending on the speed of the implantation procedure, 3–6 sets of instruments may be needed for each tagging session. Alternately, successive surgeries can be separated by at least 10 minutes to allow for appropriate contact time with the disinfectant, or the appropriate number of instrument sets can be sterilized so that a single set is used for each fish. The later approach eliminates the need for instrument rotation and disinfection, but is more expensive.

Recovery containers: Recovery containers are used to hold fish immediately after surgery. Depending on the study design, these containers also may be used to hold fish during the post-tag holding period, and then be transported to the release location. This approach is ideal, and is the assumed approach in the SOP narratives because it limits the number of fish transfers. Our general procedure is to use commercially available 19-L buckets as recovery containers. We recommend selecting a color that is dark enough to restrict light penetration (that is, avoid white), but light enough to avoid absorbing significant amounts of solar radiation, leading to risk of elevated water temperatures (that is, avoid black); we use green. Lids that fit securely on these containers are readily available and are needed to minimize disturbance.

In this SOP, because the recovery containers are used for post-tag holding, we perforate the side of the containers (fig. 7) to allow water exchange when they are immersed in a tank. The containers are only perforated in their upper portion so that they retain a 7-L volume for fish when the containers are not immersed in a larger reservoir or tank.

Figure 7. A perforated 19-liter recovery container. The bottom of the container is not perforated so that the reservoir holds 7-liters of water.

Immediately prior to starting the tagging operation, fill several recovery containers with source water and position them near the tagging station. Avoid filling the containers too far in advance of the tagging operation in order to prevent loss of water-quality. We recommend a container labeling system that allows you to record the identity of each fish placed into each recovery container.

The DO concentration in recovery containers should be 120–150 percent saturation. This increased DO concentration is critical to assisting fish recovery from the oxygen debt incurred during anesthesia. The increased DO concentration can be established using an oxygen cylinder and a diffuser.

Careful monitoring is required to ensure that the high concentration of DO is maintained in all recovery containers until the containers are put in a tank for the post-tag holding period.

A recovery process must be established for source fish that are deemed unsuitable for tagging. Fish that may be rejected from tagging include fish that do not meet the size criteria, fish that respond poorly to anesthesia, or fish that experience excessive handling or stress during the tagging process (for example, fish may have been dropped or may have jumped out of containers). Rejected fish should be set aside during the tagging operation and then released or euthanized, as directed by study objectives and scientific permits. A 19-L container should be filled with approximately 10 L of source water, labeled "reject," covered with a lid, and positioned near the tagging operation. Because a single container will be used throughout the tagging operation, equip the container with a battery-operated aerator to ensure that DO concentrations remain near saturation.

Anesthetic: Anesthetic should be added to 10-L of source water in a 19-L container. Effective working concentrations of MS-222® for juvenile salmonids are in the range of 50–90 mg/L. The exact anesthetic concentration for a tagging session should be based on the induction and recovery times of fish. Individual fish often have varied responses to MS-222®, so several fish must be monitored in order to evaluate the effectiveness of a given concentration at a given water temperature. Start with a low dose of anesthetic (for example, 60 mg/L), monitor fish response, and make adjustments as needed (see section, "Anesthetizing Fish"). Following the addition of anesthetic, add an equal amount of sodium bicarbonate to buffer the solution. Approximately 10 mL of diluted Stress Coat® should be added to the anesthesia container to protect and to restore the mucus layer of tagged fish. To provide guidance for future tagging sessions, record the anesthetic concentration used for each tagging session (or each group of fish within a session), along with the water temperature.

A maintenance dose of anesthetic is delivered to the fish's gills during surgery through a gravity feed or pump irrigation system. The fish initially is exposed to a relatively high dose of MS-222® to induce deep anesthesia. Following loss of equilibrium, the fish is moved to the surgery platform and the tagging procedure is started. During the procedure, the anesthesia is maintained by delivering a light dose of anesthetic through the irrigation system. Add 2 mL of MS-222® to the 10 L of source water in the gravity feed container, and add 2 mL of sodium bicarbonate solution as a buffer. Connect the tubing from the water source to the tagging station.

Communication among tagging personnel is critical during anesthesia preparation to ensure that anesthetic is not administered to the same container repeatedly or not at all. Our general procedure allows only one person to administer anesthetic in all needed containers to avoid confusion.

The solution in the anesthesia container should be changed periodically to minimize dilution of the working concentration of anesthesia (when fish are added) and to prevent water temperature changes of more than 2°C from the source water. Similarly, water in the gravity feed containers should be changed regularly to prevent water temperature differences and to ensure that irrigation can continue throughout a surgery without interruption. For general guidance, we recommend changing the anesthesia and gravity feed containers after 5–6 surgeries have been completed.

Anesthetizing Fish

Fish must be handled carefully and monitored closely while undergoing anesthesia. To ensure effective determination of the stage of anesthesia and the anesthesia exposure time, fish are processed individually. The process begins by carefully removing a fish from the pre-tag holding container and placing it directly in an anesthesia container. The container lid is immediately positioned and a timer is started to document exposure time. Induction time to stage 4–5 anesthesia will vary, but generally should be 2–4 minutes (average of about 3 minutes) if the appropriate concentration is used. Remove the container lid after approximately 1 minute to monitor the stage of anesthesia. Fish that lose equilibrium within the first minute of exposure to anesthesia are assumed to be especially sensitive to the anesthetic and are not used for tagging. These fish should be removed from the anesthesia container and placed in the reject container for recovery and later handling. Typically, at 1 minute of exposure, fish are partially responsive to stimuli and oriented. Once the fish loses equilibrium (estimated to be about 3 minutes), its condition should be examined. Keep the fish submerged during the exam, and look for fungus, descaling, injury, signs of disease, or other factors that would eliminate the fish from consideration for tagging (for example, an existing mark or tag). Fish that are not acceptable for tagging should be transferred to the reject container. If fish are acceptable for tagging, they are removed from the anesthesia container using a gloved hand or a net, and transferred to the balance or measuring board. A timer is started when they are removed from the anesthesia container to record the amount of time they are held in air to complete the surgery. Fish that are exposed to MS-222® for 5 minutes or longer prior to surgery are not acceptable for tagging because of the risk of medullary collapse and mortality (Mulford, 1984; Summerfelt and Smith, 1990).

The need for a change in the anesthetic concentration should be determined based on the responses of the first few fish to undergo anesthesia. If after anesthetizing several fish, you find that they are losing equilibrium too quickly (<1 minute) or too slowly (>3.5–4 minutes), or if their recovery time is extensive (>10 minutes), the anesthesia concentration should be changed. We recommend small changes in the anesthesia concentration and continued monitoring. For example, if 60 mg/L MS-222® results in slow induction times, adjust the concentration to 65 mg/L and process another group of fish before changing to 70 mg/L. Recording the anesthesia concentration used during each tagging session can provide a reference for taggers when making a decision on the initial concentration to use.

More than one anesthesia container may be useful, depending on the scale and pace of the tagging operation. Add a container for each tagger used in the tagging session. In addition, taggers that perform the surgery rapidly may have greater efficiency with an additional anesthesia container, considering that each container holds a single fish. Adding anesthesia containers holds some risk in that any delay in removing the fish and starting the surgery (that is, the previous surgery is not yet complete) may result in the fish being rejected if the exposure time is more than 5 minutes.

Measuring Fish Size

Fish morphometrics are recorded after anesthesia and before tagging. First, fish are transferred from the anesthesia container to the measuring board. The fork length (FL) of the fish is the distance from the snout to the fork in the caudal fin, and it is measured to the nearest millimeter. Following the FL measurement, the fish is transferred to a weigh boat on a scale. Ensure that the scale is properly zeroed to account for the weight of the weigh boat before the fish is added. Measure and record fish weight to the nearest 0.1 g. Both the measuring board and the weigh boat should be kept moist to reduce damage to the fish's skin. This is accomplished through the regular addition of diluted Stress Coat® to these surfaces.

Fish transfers should be done by cradling fish in two gloved hands while moving quickly and carefully. Position the measuring board and scale close to the anesthesia container to facilitate the transfers. Although the fish are anesthetized, there is a risk that fish will be dropped. If a fish is dropped to the floor it must be rejected, but if a fish is dropped a shorter distance (for example, from the handler to the tagging platform), it should be tagged unless there is an obvious injury.

The tagger generally completes the morphometric data collection, but this will vary with the size of the tagging operation. We encourage taggers to weigh and measure the fish themselves, rather than use an assistant, because doing so gives taggers insights into the fish's condition and level of anesthesia.

The first full view of the fish comes on the measuring board, and this is a good time to complete a secondary inspection of fish condition before time is spent performing a surgery. If the measuring or weighing steps are difficult to complete because of the activity level of the fish, then the level of anesthesia is too shallow to proceed with surgery. To grant these benefits while maintaining efficiency in the tagging operation, we recommend using a dedicated data recorder. The tagger can then measure and weigh the fish and verbally relay the information to the data recorder. The recorder should then log the measurements on the datasheet and repeat the data back to the tagger to avoid any miscommunication and to allow for corrections.

Implantation of Transmitters

Irrigation: Immediately after the morphometric data have been collected, the fish should be placed on the surgery platform, ventral side up, and irrigation should be established. Place the irrigation tubing in the mouth of the fish and ensure consistent water flow over the gills. Inadequate flow through the irrigation system will cause the fish to become agitated, which can mimic a shallow depth of anesthesia. Excessive flow through the irrigation system can push overflow water toward the incision area and, therefore, should be avoided.

The irrigation system is configured to deliver sedation (a low concentration dose of anesthetic), freshwater, or a combination of both. Fish should receive sedation at the start of the surgery, but as the procedure continues, the sedation should be reduced to begin the recovery process. At approximately the mid-point of the surgery, the tagger should consider providing irrigation water that is an equal mix of sedation and freshwater. When the surgery is almost completed, we recommend switching the irrigation to fresh water. The tagger must monitor the level of anesthesia throughout the surgery and make adjustments to the irrigation flow to manage the level of anesthesia, as needed.

Incision: The incision is made near the pelvic girdle, using a micro scalpel. Locate the pelvic girdle of the fish by visual exam and palpation. In a ventral view, the pelvic girdle has a "V" or "U" shape, with the single point oriented anteriorly (toward the head) (fig. 8). The most anterior point of the pelvic girdle is the positioning guide for the location of the incision. Using a micro scalpel, make an incision about 3 mm anterior to the anterior point of the pelvic girdle, and about 3 mm away from and parallel to the mid-ventral line. Draw the blade toward the head of the fish as the incision is lengthened to avoid damaging the pelvic girdle.

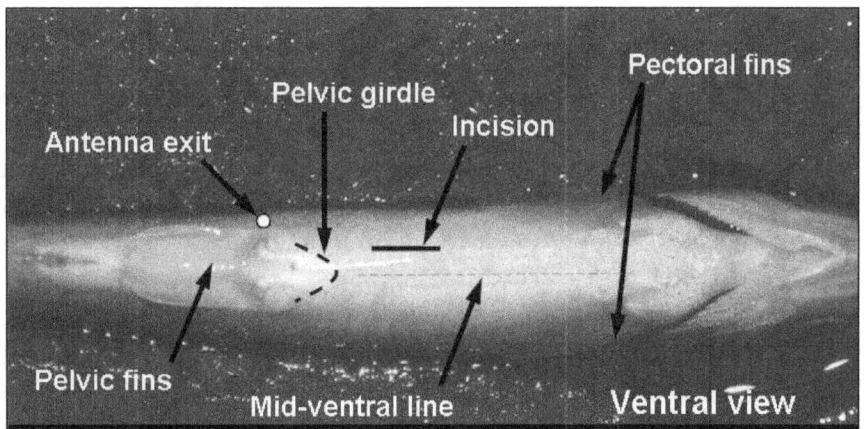

Figure 8. Ventral view of a juvenile salmon on a tagging platform. Locations of the pelvic girdle, incision, and antenna exit site are shown.

The incision should be only long enough to allow insertion of the transmitter without tearing the adjacent tissue. A good estimate of appropriate incision length is the diameter of the transmitter because the transmitter's length can be inserted through the incision after its head has entered the body. A short incision will minimize risk of organ damage, reduce the area vulnerable to infection, minimize tissue damage due to sutures, and reduce the time needed for closure. The incision should be deep enough to penetrate the peritoneum (the thin membrane separating the abdominal cavity from the musculature) without damaging internal organs. The spleen and pyloric caeca are often located near the incision, so the incision must be made carefully (see fig. 9).

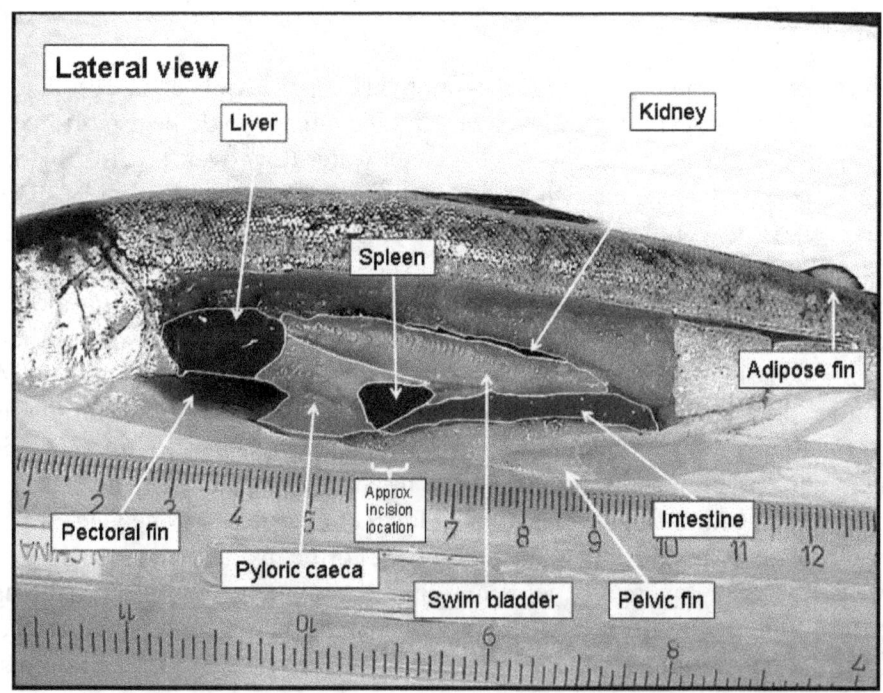

Figure 9.   Lateral view of a juvenile salmon with location of structures and organs and approximate location of the surgical incision.

The optimal incision has clearly defined wound margins that will promote complete apposition and healing. Ideally, the incision will be completed with a single pass of the micro scalpel rather than the use of a "sawing" motion. If, after several fish, the tagger finds that multiple passes with the scalpel are needed to penetrate the peritoneum, a longer micro scalpel should be considered. Because a single micro scalpel will be used on several fish, it is important to monitor scalpel effectiveness to determine the timing for replacement. If the blade fails to move smoothly through the tissue or requires additional pressure to make the incision, it should be replaced.

After the incision has been made, use forceps to open the incision to quickly evaluate effectiveness and any potential organ damage. Insert the forceps into the incision to ensure that the peritoneum was penetrated along the full length of the incision and that there is clear access to the body cavity. Assess any potential organ damage by looking for bleeding. The spleen is located near the incision site and will cause significant bleeding if damaged. If the fish is bleeding excessively, it should not be implanted with a transmitter. The rejected fish may be sutured without a transmitter and recovered for release or sacrificed, depending on study design and scientific permit authority.

Transmitter antenna: If the transmitter has an antenna, an antenna exit site must be made in the lateral body wall so that the antenna can exit the body and trail behind the fish as it swims. We use a modified shielded needle technique (Ross and Kleiner, 1982) where a plastic catheter is positioned over the point of a needle so that it cannot damage organs as it is guided through the abdominal cavity. Following purchase, the catheter typically must be modified slightly to function as a shield. The non-tapered end of the catheter typically has a plastic tip with a connector, and this part of the catheter should be removed (fig. 10).

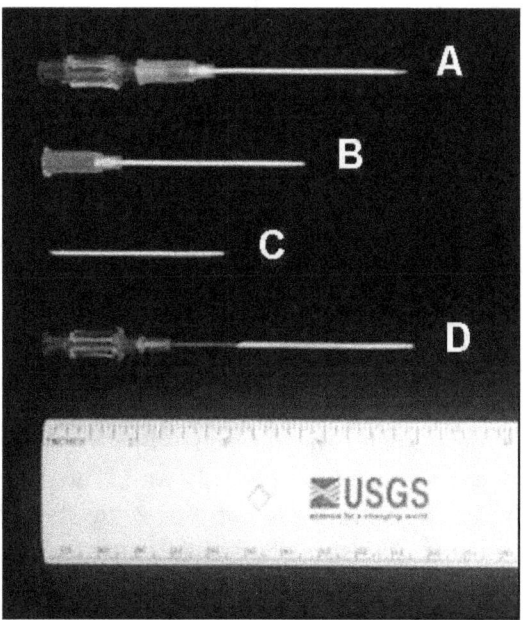

Figure 10. Example catheters used to perform a shielded needle technique to create an exit location for a trailing antenna on a radio transmitter. Image A shows the needle and catheter combination as it comes packaged from the manufacturer. The pink catheter tip (shown in B) must be removed (as in C) prior to use. The modified catheter is then positioned over the needle (D) as it will be used during surgical procedures.

Insert the shielded needle (catheter covering the tip of the needle) into the abdominal cavity through the incision and guide it to the antenna exit site. Hold the shielded needle between thumb and forefinger, keeping the needle tip covered by the catheter to protect the organs. The antenna exit site position should be even with the insertion of the pelvic fins on the longitudinal axis of the fish, and should be about 40 percent of the distance from the mid-ventral line to the lateral line on the vertical axis of the fish (fig. 11).

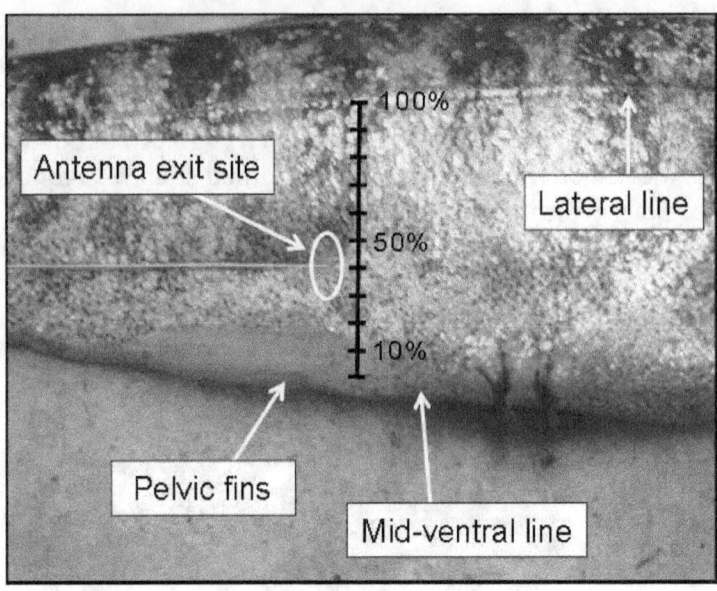

Figure 11. Lateral, external view of a juvenile salmon with the location for the antenna exit site.

After the catheter is positioned at the antenna exit site, draw back the catheter to expose the tip of the needle, and use the needle to puncture the body wall. The orientation of the tip of the needle is important for a clean puncture. The cutting edge of the needle should be facing away from the body wall (see fig. 12). If the cutting edge is against the body wall, the needle may scrape along the peritoneum rather than make a clean cut. Depending on the manufacturer, there is usually a tab or other mark on the shaft end of the needle that can be used as a landmark to indicate the orientation of the cutting edge. Prior to puncturing the body wall, be certain that the catheter is withdrawn far enough along the length of the needle to expose the tip. If the catheter is covering the tip of the needle during the puncture through the body wall, the puncture wound will be larger and more irregular and healing may be delayed. Following the puncture of the body wall, advance the catheter through the wound so that it is visible from the outside of the fish.

Hold the catheter in position, extending out the incision anteriorly and the exit wound posteriorly, and withdraw the needle. The catheter now forms a channel that allows the antenna to be threaded through the incision to the antenna exit site.

Route the transmitter antenna through the catheter, starting at the incision. Keep the body of the transmitter in your gloved hand to avoid it contacting the surface of the fish or other surfaces where it could become contaminated. After the transmitter antenna has exited the lateral body wall, pull the catheter out of the body wall and off the free (non-transmitter) end of the antenna.

There is no exact specification as to what diameter or length of catheter to use. The catheter with the smallest diameter that will accommodate the transmitter antenna is optimal because it will minimize the size of the exit wound. In our experience, a 20-gauge needle will accommodate most transmitter antennas. The length of the needle may be limiting, however, based on fish length. The needle and catheter need to be long enough to bridge the distance between the incision and the exit site. Needles and catheters can be used for several surgeries and should be disinfected between surgeries along with the other surgical instruments. The tapered end of the catheter will begin to fray or bend and the cutting edge of the needle becomes dull after repeated use, so they should be replaced at regular intervals.

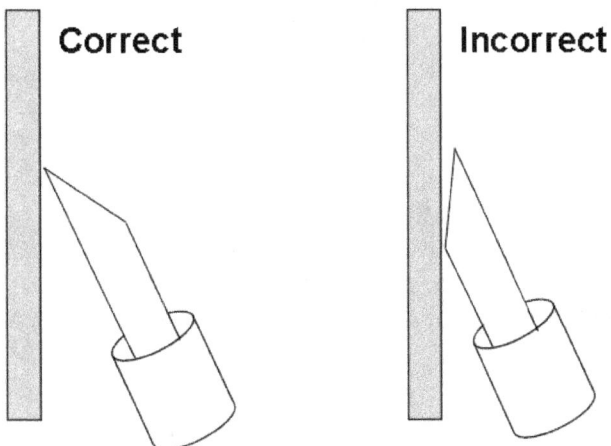

Figure 12. Schematic showing the correct and incorrect orientation of the tip of the needle against the body wall when the shielded needle technique is used to create an antenna exit site.

Transmitter insertion: Orient the transmitter vertically, and carefully insert it in the body cavity through the incision. If there is resistance during insertion, suggesting that the transmitter may tear the tissue at the edges of the incision, the incision should be enlarged.

Once inserted, position the transmitter directly beneath the incision. This positioning will protect organs during incision closure because the suture needle will contact the transmitter rather than any organs.

If additional tags will be used, insert them through the incision. For some study designs, PIT tags are used in conjunction with radio or acoustic transmitters. All tags should be tested for proper function and disinfected prior to implantation.

Incision closure: Two sutures, in a simple interrupted pattern, are used to close the incision. The simple interrupted pattern (fig. 13) is used because it involves independent closure efforts. This suture pattern ensures that the integrity of the entire incision (and corresponding risk of transmitter loss) will not be affected if one of the sutures becomes loose or untied. A modified surgeon's (or friction) knot is used to secure each suture. The knot consists of three double-wrap throws (that is, a single wrap of the suture material around the surgical instrument) and is commonly described as a 2 × 3 knot (2 wraps on each of 3 throws). The direction of the wraps should be alternated between throws to aid knot security. For example, on the first throw, the direction of the wrap is away from the tagger, on the second throw, the wrap is towards the tagger, and on the third throw, the wrap is again away from the tagger. The first throw should be lightly tensioned, so that the edges of the incision are drawn closely together (are well apposed) but do not overlap. The second and third throws have less impact on the apposition of the sides of the incision and can therefore be applied with increased tension to aid knot security. Ensure that the wraps from each throw lie flat and do not twist on themselves and form a ball.

After the knot is complete, cut the suture so that the tag ends of the knot are about 3 mm long. The length of suture tag ends should be long enough to ensure the integrity of the knot, but as short as possible to reduce the available surface area for bacterial or fungal growth.

The suture needle entry and exit sites should be about 2 mm from the edge of the incision. This distance is sufficient to anchor the suture material and to resist the tendency of the suture to pull through the entry or exit site, tearing the tissue in a line perpendicular to the incision. When entry and exit sites are positioned farther from the incision the knot is less effective at creating and maintaining good apposition of the sides of the incision. Locking the suture needle in the jaws of the needle holder may allow the best control during needle entry and exit.

Ideally, the sutures should penetrate the full depth of the body wall and peritoneum. The incision will heal best when the full thickness of the body wall (including the peritoneum) on both sides of the incision is pulled into apposition. Examination of the internal aspect of sutures, looking to confirm penetration of the peritoneum, is an important part of developing surgical proficiency.

The two sutures should be positioned with equal spacing along the length of the incision. The goal is to have approximately equal distance between the two sutures as well as between each suture and the adjacent edge of the incision. For example, with a 6-mm incision, sutures should be positioned 2 mm from each other and 2 mm from the anterior and posterior margins of the incision (fig. 13). A third suture may be added if needed to adequately close the incision. The need for a third suture will depend on the length of the incision (which depends on the size of the transmitter) and the placement of the first two sutures. Although adding a third suture poses some additional risks (for example, infection and tearing) compared to a well-closed incision with two sutures, the addition is warranted if there is risk of transmitter loss due to a partially open incision.

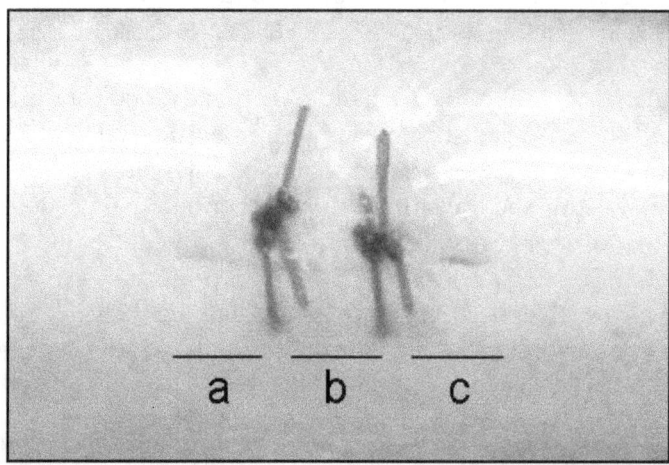

Figure 13. Two simple interrupted sutures. Note the suture positioning, where distances a, b, and c are approximately equal.

There is no exact specification for suture size. The general recommendation is to use the smallest diameter suture material that will secure the incision without tearing through the adjacent tissue. Typically a 4–0 suture is used for fish weighing more than about 50 g, and a 5–0 suture is used for fish weighing less than about 50 g.

Reduce sedation exposure: If the ventilation rate of the fish has been slow and regular throughout the surgical procedure, consider irrigating with fresh water to begin the recovery from anesthesia. A good time to switch to freshwater irrigation is after the completion of the first suture, as the second suture generally can be completed quickly and effectively, even while the fish is beginning to revive. An alternate approach is to continue to provide sedation through the gravity feed and to open the valve for the freshwater gravity feed container. This approach reduces the sedation concentration by approximately one-half. Full sedation can be continued for fish that have been active on the surgery platform during the initial phases of surgery.

Rotate instruments: A single set of surgical instruments should be used for a given surgical procedure and adequately disinfected prior to use in subsequent procedures. Prior to the surgery, the instruments should be removed from the disinfectant tray and placed into a rinse tray filled with distilled or deionized water. Following use, instruments should be returned to the disinfectant tray. A new tray is then selected for the next procedure to allow sufficient exposure time to the disinfectant. Heavy organic debris (for example, scales and blood) should be removed from instruments prior to disinfection. Small toothbrushes are useful for this purpose. Rotate unused portions of suture (along with the attached needle) with a given set of instruments so that they are effectively disinfected.

Disinfectant and rinse trays should be replaced regularly during a tagging session. Organic debris will accumulate in the disinfectant tray through multiple surgeries (reducing effectiveness of the disinfectant) and the solution will be diluted slowly as instruments are moved between the rinse tray and the disinfectant. Replace the water in the rinse trays as needed to be sure they are effectively removing all disinfectant residues.

Record special conditions: Although most surgeries will proceed as planned, there likely will be a few surgeries where atypical conditions arise. For example, the micro scalpel may begin to dull so the incision is somewhat irregular. Perhaps a third suture may be used or the fish may show some bleeding. These situations with individual fish should be recorded because they may be linked with wound healing, behavior, or survival. Additionally, analysis of the frequency of such events might guide modifications to tagging procedures in future studies. Consider having a field on the datasheet where generalized comments can be recorded.

Post-Tag Recovery

After the surgical procedure is complete, fish are transferred from the surgery platform to a recovery container. The transfer is performed by holding the fish in position on the surgery platform and carrying the platform to the recovery container. This approach eliminates the need to pick up the fish from the platform and reduces the risk that the fish will be dropped during the transfer. If a fish is dropped to the floor after it is tagged, it should be euthanized, and the transmitter should be removed, disinfected, and implanted into another fish.

As soon as a tagged fish is placed in a recovery container, the container cover is positioned and the timer recording air exposure time is stopped. The air exposure time for each fish is recorded and is a good indicator of the risk of stress to the fish because it measures the amount of time the fish was exposed to air, not just the time needed to complete the surgical procedure.

The density in recovery containers should not exceed 10 g of fish per L of water. Depending on the size of the fish, this generally translates to 2–3 fish per 19-L recovery container (the containers are not full of water due to the perforations). This is a highly conservative density level, designed to optimize holding conditions for tagged fish.

Recovery containers are maintained at increased DO concentrations to help fish recover from the oxygen debt incurred during anesthesia. Because the recovery containers are closed systems (no water exchange) the increased DO concentrations can readily be maintained for short time periods. Fish should remain in the high DO saturation environment for at least 10 minutes to allow them to regain equilibrium and to demonstrate at least nominal swimming activity. Use a timer to record recovery time for each container of tagged fish. The timer should record the minimum recovery time for the group of fish in the container; therefore, it should be started when the last fish is placed in the container. The first fish placed into the container will have a slightly longer recovery time.

Fish generally regain equilibrium in 3–5 minutes (depending on water temperature, anesthesia exposure, and individual sensitivity). Fish that take more than about 5 minutes to regain equilibrium require close monitoring. Fish that do not show regular ventilation rates, are not readily recovering from surgery, or both should be manually ram ventilated to increase the flow of oxygenated water over the gills. Ram ventilation is accomplished by grasping the fish gently and moving them forward and back within the recovery container. The increased water flow over the gills will increase and stabilize the heart rate, which leads to increased blood flow to the gills to help eliminate the anesthesia (Ross and Ross, 2008). Tagged fish that do not recover well, even with assistance, or for other reasons are determined to be inappropriate for release, should be euthanized. The transmitter should be removed, de-activated, and disinfected or sterilized for later use.

After fish regain equilibrium and show responsiveness to stimuli, the recovery container is moved to a post-tagging holding tank. The perforations in the recovery containers allow exchange with tank water to enable the maintenance of water-quality during the holding period.

Release of Tagged Fish

The last opportunity a researcher has to visually examine tagged fish is immediately prior to release. This is the time to assess whether fish are behaving as expected and whether they are appropriate subjects for the telemetry study. Examine all post-tag holding containers for dead fish, moribund fish, and shed transmitters. The exam should be conducted with as little disturbance as possible. The lid of the container should be partially removed, just enough for the fish to be visible. Try to avoid letting significant amounts of light into the container as fish will likely jump and may escape.

Observe fish condition by noting swimming activity and the vertical position of fish in the container. Carefully remove moribund, dead, or poorly performing fish so as not to disturb the other fish in the container. Stressors, such as chasing the fish immediately prior to release, may induce a stress response that could influence fish behavior or survival. Remove the transmitters from fish that will not be released and record the final condition of the individual tagged fish.

We recommend that transmitter function be validated immediately prior to the release of tagged fish. This step is valuable because transmitters may have failed after exposure to water, or there may have been errors during the activation procedure. Monitoring equipment (radio or acoustic telemetry receivers) will be needed, and several approaches can be used, but they are outside the scope of this SOP.

The final step in the tagging procedure is to release tagged fish from their holding containers so they can be monitored. If transportation is required to move fish from the post-tag holding location to the release location, be sure to maintain water-quality standards and access to the air-water interface during transport. It is useful and convenient to document water temperature during transport with a thermograph. These devices are readily available and inexpensive. Place one in the transport container to monitor temperature changes during the transport effort. Review the data and make any necessary modifications to the transport procedures to ensure compliance with water-quality standards. In addition to water-quality, it is important to maintain fish access to the air-water interface during transport because rough handling can cause fish to expel air and become negatively buoyant. Fish that cannot maintain neutral buoyancy likely will show altered behavior, such as variable depth profiles or delayed movements.

After tagged fish arrive at the release location, put the holding containers in or near the water and let tagged fish volitionally swim out of the container. Record the release time for individual tagged fish or for the groups of fish within each holding container.

Clean-Up and Disinfection

Surplus fish: Source fish that were not needed for tagging and fish that were deemed inappropriate for the tagging operation need to be released, returned, or euthanized. Reference the appropriate collection or handling permit or use local guidance to determine the best course of action for surplus fish. Record the numbers of surplus fish to help refine fish needs for future tagging operations.

Discard tagging solutions: The chlorhexidine and anesthetic solutions used during the tagging operation should be discarded based on local guidance and label instructions. The MS-222® solutions commonly are poured onto pavement or gravel surfaces for evaporation or filtration. The chlorhexidine solution may be handled like MS-222® or may be discarded through any water system that receives wastewater treatment. For settings where disposal may be challenging, chlorhexidine can be collected during the tagging operation and transported to a facility for disposal. Full solution capture generally is not an option for MS-222® because of the high volume of solution used during a tagging operation.

Clean and disinfect: Surgical instruments, working surfaces, and holding containers need to be cleaned and disinfected regularly. At the end of each tagging operation, surgical instruments should be cleaned and prepared for sterilization. Discard any open or partially used suture packets and micro scalpel blades in a sharps container. If catheters were used, discard the plastic catheter as it cannot be sterilized. The needle portion can be retained and packaged with the instruments. Use a small toothbrush to scrub organic debris off all surgical instruments. Pay close attention to the jaws of the needle drivers and the forceps where organic matter is most likely to accumulate. Rinse and dry all instruments. Consider an application of an instrument lubricant to enhance instrument performance and longevity. Wrap instruments in a cloth or place them in an autoclave bag to prepare them for sterilization. Apply autoclave tape or another marker system so that sterilization can be confirmed prior to the next use of the instruments. Consider wrapping each complete instrument set individually to speed the set-up of the next tagging operation.

All working surfaces and tagging equipment should be disinfected. Spray countertops, the tagging platform, the tagging station, nets, and any other working surfaces with Virkon® Aquatic solution. Alternately, a large container of disinfectant solution can be used so that equipment can be soaked. Allow 10 minutes of contact time and rinse with clean water. Position equipment to drain, and allow a thorough drying prior to the next use.

Clean and disinfect all water and holding containers regularly. The need for cleaning and disinfection will depend on the level of use and local water-quality. Tanks should be scrubbed and disinfected when the sediment load is sufficient to influence water-quality. Anesthesia, reject, recovery, and gravity feed containers should be disinfected weekly if the tagging operation occurs daily. Disinfect containers by applying Virkon® Aquatic, allowing 10 minutes of contact time, rinsing, and allowing containers to drain and dry.

Recommendations

Maximize Efficiency

The procedures for surgical implantation of transmitters in juvenile salmonids can be used in any tagging operation, regardless of scale. A small-scale tagging operation may involve a tagger, an assistant, and potentially a dedicated data recorder. A larger operation may involve multiple taggers and numerous support personnel. The scale of the tagging effort will depend on the number of fish that will be tagged during a single tagging session (that is, the tagging load). Regardless of the scale of the tagging operation, our recommendation is to maximize efficiency by adopting some simple procedures and providing appropriate support staff. When the tagging load is high or the timing is particularly critical (for example, tagging groups of fish to be released hourly), the tagging operation must operate efficiently. There is no downside to introducing efficiency into smaller scale tagging operations; efficiency is just less critical in these circumstances. The largest source of inefficiency in a tagging operation is the delay in starting a surgery because a fish is not yet anesthetized. If the tagger is ready to perform the surgery and the fish is not ready to be removed from the anesthesia container, minutes of delay are incurred for each fish. Because a proficient tagger can weigh, measure, and tag a fish in about 3 minutes, waiting 2 minutes for anesthesia is a significant delay. This delay is readily managed by providing a dedicated assistant to the tagger who can move source fish into anesthesia and deliver them to the tagging area. Close coordination between the tagger and the assistant is required. The tagger should request that a fish be added to the anesthesia container before the previous fish has been removed from the surgery platform. The exact timing will depend on the proficiency and speed of the tagger, but a general rule is for taggers to request a new fish once the first suture has been tied on their current fish. Using this approach, the taggers have sufficient time between surgeries to rotate their instruments, to prepare the next set of instruments, to conduct a quick exam of the fish in the anesthesia container, and to begin the next procedure.

Providing appropriate support staff is another approach to improving efficiency. A dedicated data recorder keeps the tagging operation running smoothly because the person is constantly available to record tagger comments and to assist with monitoring anesthesia and preparing surgery materials. When multiple taggers are used simultaneously, we recommend that each tagger have a dedicated data recorder.

Monitor and Document SOP Compliance

We recommend that compliance with the SOP be monitored and documented. Staff can "drift" from the protocol through time, especially when more than a few people are involved in tagging operations. To control protocol drift across time or personnel, researchers should draft a checklist of measurable SOP elements, such as DO concentrations or water temperatures and use it to conduct compliance inspections. An example checklist for such inspections is provided in appendix C. Complete several inspections over the course of the study so that all staff involved in tagging operations are included in at least one inspection. Reporting of study findings should include full details of the SOP and a summary of the findings from the compliance inspections.

Evaluate Transmitter Effects

Researchers should consider evaluating transmitter effects in a controlled setting to support the collection of telemetry data on study animals. There are various approaches that can be used to evaluate the risk of transmitter effects, ranging from monitoring simple outcomes, such as mortality and transmitter loss, to more complex evaluations, such as swimming performance or predator avoidance ability. An overview of procedures that can be used to conduct evaluations of transmitter effects is available in Liedtke and Wargo-Rub (2012). The ideal evaluation would use the same personnel, fish source, and procedures as were used for the field telemetry study so that their influence on the fish can be documented. An easily performed approach is to surgically implant transmitters in fish and then hold them under controlled conditions for the duration of the expected transmitter battery life. Inactive or "dummy" transmitters can be used as long as they accurately reflect the weight and external material, size, and shape of active transmitters. Check for mortalities and shed transmitters regularly and monitor general fish condition. This type of evaluation, even with a few fish, provides compelling evidence about the likely fate of fish released for the telemetry study.

Report Methods in Detail

Researchers should report, in detail, the procedures used for transmitter implantation and the training and experience of the taggers. We encourage rigor in reporting of procedures such as pre-tag and post-tag holding, fish handling, and efforts toward aseptic technique. The skill of the tagger can have a significant effect on the outcome of the tagging procedure (Wagner and Cooke, 2005), so the number of taggers, their contribution to the study effort, and their experience and training should be reported in detail.

Recapture Tagged Fish

Finally, we recommend that researchers take advantage of any opportunities that arise to examine tagged fish after they have been released. The use of a secondary mark (for example, PIT tag, fin clip, or a non-electronic tag) will aid this effort, especially in the event of shed transmitters. Fish may be incidentally recaptured through recreational or commercial harvest or purposefully recaptured by first locating the tagged fish using the transmitter signal and then netting or electroshocking to recover it (Jepsen and others, 2000, 2002; Koed and Thorstad, 2001; Jepsen, 2003). In some cases, the fish may not be physically recaptured, but may be detected by researchers conducting video surveillance.

Regardless of the means, recapture provides an opportunity to evaluate, in a real life setting, the effectiveness of the surgical implantation procedure. Conduct both external and internal exams on recaptured fish, looking for tissue or organ damage, infection, healing, and location of the transmitter relative to the original placement. Document findings with photography, and provide detailed descriptions during study reporting. Negative outcomes of transmitter attachment procedures are rarely reported, but they provide valuable insight. For example, based on recaptured fish, Bauer and others (2005) found that the location of the exit site for a trailing antenna had migrated 3 cm, and Thorstad and others (2001) described a transmitter antenna that had accumulated significant biofouling.

Summary

Surgical implantation procedures have become a common tool for fisheries applications. Surgical techniques generally are reported with few details, however, limiting the learning opportunities for surgeons. Most fish surgeons learned their techniques and choose their materials based on the experience of colleagues who have performed surgeries or through their own trial-and-error process (Cooke and Wagner, 2004). There are diverse opinions on the most appropriate surgical techniques and materials (for example, suture material, knot, and suture pattern), and they generally are aggressively defended, despite the potential lack of experimental evidence supporting them. This Standard Operating Procedure (SOP) does not purport to describe the single best set of procedures for surgical implantation of transmitters in juvenile salmonids. The purpose of the SOP is to share the procedures that have allowed the Columbia River Research Laboratory to implant transmitters into large numbers of fish with very high survival rates and very low transmitter losses. We believe that this SOP is sound, as it has been rigorously tested in field settings with large numbers of fish, taggers with varied skill levels, variable fish sizes and species, and a range of environmental conditions (for example, water temperature, dissolved oxygen, and total dissolved gas). Additionally, the SOP has been used to evaluate fish performance and transmitter effects in laboratory studies. Because there is no single tagging SOP that will fit all situations, each researcher must adopt procedures and materials that are defensible based on their experimental evidence, experience, or the scientific literature.

This SOP can be applied as published, or modified to fit specific study objectives or site logistics. We commonly make minor adjustments to fit new applications, while maintaining the guiding principles and details of the procedures. Although the SOP details procedures specific to juvenile salmon, many of the principles apply generally to fish surgeries and can be used to develop SOPs for other species or life stages.

Good fish-handling practices are an overarching theme in the SOP because we believe they are integrally linked with good surgical outcome. Fish-handling procedures generally are underemphasized in descriptions of surgical techniques because of the focus on the details of the surgery itself. Good surgical performance certainly contributes to a good outcome, but we believe that the effects of poor fish handling or poorly managed anesthesia can quickly outweigh the benefits of excellent surgical technique. In our experience, good fish handling, combined with a well-executed tagger training program and sound aseptic technique, will produce consistently positive surgical outcomes.

Acknowledgments

The development and refinement of this SOP would not have been possible without the assistance of a large group of Columbia River Research Laboratory staff. This work represents the efforts of a large group of people over a number of years. Special thanks to Noah Adams, Tim Counihan, Brian Ekstrom, Jill Hardiman, Russell Perry, Dennis Rondorf, Collin Smith, Jamie Sprando, Ryan Tomka, Israel Duran, Leah Sullivan, and Jill Cole. David Hand, Brian Hayes, and Lynne Casal helped greatly during the review and formatting of the document.

References Cited

Adams, N.S., Rondorf, D.W., Evans, S.D., Kelly, J.E., and Perry, R.W., 1998a, Effects of surgically and gastrically implanted radio transmitters on growth and feeding behavior of juvenile Chinook salmon: Transactions of the American Fisheries Society, v. 127, p. 128–136.

Adams, N.S., Rondorf, D.W., Evans, S.D., Kelly, J.E., and Perry, R.W., 1998b, Effects of surgically and gastrically implanted radio transmitters on swimming performance and predator avoidance of juvenile Chinook salmon (*Oncorhynchus tshawytscha*): Canadian Journal of Fisheries and Aquatic Sciences, v. 55, p. 781–787.

American Fisheries Society, 2004, Guidelines for the use of fishes in research: Bethesda Maryland, American Fisheries Society Press.

Bauer, C., Unfer, G., and Loupal, G., 2005, Potential problems with external trailing antennae— Antenna migration and ingrowth of epithelial tissue, a case study from a recaptured *Chondrostoma nasus*: Journal of Fish Biology, v. 67, p. 885– 889.

Beeman, J.W, Kock, T.J., and Perry, R.W., 2011, Analysis of dam-passage survival of yearling and subyearling Chinook salmon and juvenile steelhead at The Dalles Dam, Oregon, 2010: U.S. Geological Survey Open-File Report 2011–1162. 38 p. (Also available at http://pubs.er.usgs.gov/publication/ofr20111162.)

Brown, R.S., Harnish, R.A., Carter, K.M., Boyd, J.W., Deters, K.A., and Eppard, M.B., 2010, An evaluation of the maximum tag burden for implantation of acoustic transmitters in juvenile Chinook salmon: North American Journal of Fisheries Management, v. 30, p. 499–505.

California Department of Water Resources, 2012, 2011 Georgiana Slough non-physical barrier performance evaluation project report: Sacramento, California Department of Water Resources, 228 p.

Cooke, S.J., Graeb, B.D.S., Suski, C.D., and Østrand, K.G., 2003, Effects of suture material on incision healing, growth, and survival of juvenile largemouth bass implanted with miniature radio transmitters—Case study of a novice and experienced fish surgeon: Journal of Fish Biology, v. 62, p. 1,366–1,380.

Cooke, S.J., and Wagner, G.N., 2004, Training, experience, and opinions of researchers who use surgical techniques to implant telemetry devices into fish: Fisheries, v. 29, p. 10– 18.

Counihan, T.D., Hardiman, J.M., Walker, C.E., Puls, A.L., and Holmberg, G.S., 2006a, Survival estimates of migrant juvenile salmonids through Bonneville Dam using radiotelemetry, 2004: Annual report prepared by U.S. Geological Survey, Cook, Washington, for the U.S. Army Corps of Engineers, Portland, Oregon, contract number W66QKZ40420056.

Counihan, T.D., Puls, A.L., Walker, C.E., Hardiman, J.M., and Holmberg, G.S., 2006b, Survival estimates of migrant juvenile salmonids through The Dalles Dam using radiotelemetry, 2004: Annual report prepared by U.S. Geological Survey, Cook, Washington, for the U.S. Army Corps of Engineers, Portland, Oregon, contract number W66QKZ40369527.

Elliott, D.G., and Pascho, R.J., 2001, Evidence that coded-wire tagging procedures can enhance transmission of *Renibacterium salmoninarum* in Chinook salmon: Journal of Aquatic Animal Health, v. 13, p. 181–193.

Flagg, T.A., and Harrell, L.W., 1990, Use of water-to-water transfers to maximize survival of salmonids stocked directly into seawater: The Progressive Fish Culturist, v. 52, p. 127– 129.

Fried, S.M, McCleave, J.D., and Stred, K.A., 1976, Buoyancy compensation by Atlantic salmon (*Salmo salar*) smolts tagged internally with dummy telemetry transmitters: Journal of the Fisheries Research Board of Canada, v. 3, p. 1,377–1,380.

Gallepp, G.W., and Magnuson, J.J., 1972, Effects of negative buoyancy on the behavior of the bluegill, *Lepomis macrochirus* Rafinesque: Transactions of the American Fisheries Society, v. 101, p. 507–512.

Hall, J.E., Chamberlin, J., Kagley, A.N., Greene, C., and Fresh, K.L., 2009, Effects of gastric and surgical insertions of dummy ultrasonic transmitters on juvenile Chinook salmon in seawater: Transactions of the American Fisheries Society, v.138, p. 52–57.

Harms, C.A., 2005, Surgery in fish research: common procedures and postoperative care: Lab Animal, v. 34, p. 28–34.

Harms, C.A., and Lewbart, G.A., 2011, The veterinarian's role in surgical implantation of electronic tags in fish: Reviews in Fish Biology and Fisheries, v. 21. p. 25–33.

Harvey, H.H., Hoar, W.S., and Brothers, C.R., 1968, Sounding response of the kokanee and sockeye salmon: Journal of the Fisheries Research Board of Canada, v. 25, p. 1,115–1,131.

Houston, A.H., Madden, J.A., Woods, R.J., and Miles, H.M., 1971, Some physiological effects of handling and tricaine methane sulphonate anesthetization upon the brook trout, *Salvelinus fontinalis*: Journal of the Fisheries Research Board of Canada, v. 28, p. 625–633.

Jepsen, N., 2003, Long-term retention of surgically implanted radio transmitters in pikeperch: Journal of Fish Biology, v. 63, p. 260–262.

Jepsen, N., Davis, L.E., Schreck, C.B., and Siddens, B., 2001, The physiological response of Chinook salmon smolts to two methods of radio-tagging: Transactions of the American Fisheries Society, v. 130, p. 495 – 500.

Jepsen, N., Koed, A., Thorstad, E.B., and Baras, E., 2002, Surgical implantation of telemetry transmitters in fish—How much have we learned?: Hydrobiologia, v. 483, p. 239–248.

Jepsen, N., Mikkelsen, J.S., and Koed, A., 2008, Effects of tag and suture type on survival and growth of brown trout with surgically implanted telemetry tags in the wild: Journal of Fish Biology, v. 72, p. 594–602.

Jepsen, N., Pedersen, S., and Thorstad, E., 2000, Behavioural interactions between prey (trout smolts) and predators (pike and pikeperch) in an impounded river: Regulated Rivers—Research and Management, v. 16, p. 189–198.

Kelsh, S. W., and Shields, B., 1996, Care and handling of sampled organisms, in Murphy, B.R., and Willis, D.W., eds., Fisheries techniques (2d ed.): Bethesda, Maryland, American Fisheries Society, p. 121–155.

Koed, A., and Thorstad, E.B., 2001, Long-term effect of radio-tagging on the swimming performance of pikeperch: Journal of Fish Biology, v. 58, p. 1,753–1,756.

Lacroix, G. L., Knox, D., and McCurdy, P., 2004, Effects of implanted dummy acoustic transmitters on juvenile Atlantic salmon: Transactions of the American Fisheries Society, v. 133, p. 211–220.

Liedtke, T.L., and Wargo-Rub, A.M., 2012, Techniques for telemetry transmitter attachment and evaluation of transmitter effects on fish performance, in Adams, N.S., Beeman, J.W., and Eiler, J.H., eds., Telemetry techniques—A user's guide for fisheries research: Bethesda, Maryland, American Fisheries Society, p. 45–87.

Lucas, M.C., 1989, Effects of implanted dummy transmitters on mortality, growth and tissue reaction in rainbow trout, *Salmo gairdneri* Richardson: Journal of Fish Biology, v. 35, p. 577–587.

Marking, L.L., and Meyer, F.P., 1985, Are better anesthetics needed in fisheries?: Fisheries, v. 10, no. 3, p. 2–5.

Martinelli, T. L., Hansel, H.C., and Shively, R.S., 1998, Growth and physiological responses to surgical and gastric radio transmitter implantation techniques in subyearling Chinook salmon (*Oncorhynchus tshawytscha*): Hydrobiologia, v. 371–372, p. 79–87.

Marty, G.D., and Summerfelt, R.C., 1986, Pathways and mechanisms for expulsion of surgically implanted dummy transmitters from channel catfish: Transactions of the American Fisheries Society, v. 115, p. 577–589.

Matthews, G.M., Park, D.L., Achord, S., and Ruehle, T.E., 1986, Static seawater challenge test to measure relative stress levels in spring Chinook salmon smolts: Transactions of the American Fisheries Society, v. 115, p. 236–244.

Maule, A.G., Schreck, C.B., Bradford, C.S., and Barton, B.A., 1988, Physiological effects of collecting and transporting emigrating juvenile Chinook salmon past dams on the Columbia River: Transactions of the American Fisheries Society, v. 117, p. 245–261.

Mesa, M.G., Weiland, L.K., and Maule, A.G., 2000, Progression and severity of gas bubble trauma in juvenile salmonids: Transactions of the American Fisheries Society, v. 129, p. 174–185.

Moore, A., Russell, I.C., and Potter, E.C.E., 1990, The effects of intraperitoneally implanted dummy acoustic transmitters on the behavior and physiology of juvenile Atlantic salmon, *Salmo salar* L: Journal of Fish Biology, v. 37, p. 713–721.

Mulcahy, D.M., 2003, Surgical implantation of transmitters into fish: ILAR (Institute for Laboratory Animal Research) Journal, v. 44, p. 295–306.

Mulford, C.J., 1984, Use of a surgical skin stapler to quickly close incisions in striped bass: North American Journal of Fisheries Management, v. 4, p. 571–573.

Penne, C.R., Ahrens, N.L., Summerfelt, R.C., and Pierce, C.L., 2007, Effect of relative volume on radio transmitter expulsion in subadult common carp: North American Journal of Fisheries Management, v. 27, p. 986–991.

Perry, R.W., Adams, N.S., and Rondorf, D.W., 2001, Buoyancy compensation of juvenile Chinook salmon implanted with two different size dummy transmitters: Transactions of the American Fisheries Society, v. 130, p. 46–52.

Perry, R.W., Braatz, A.C., Fielding, S.D., Lucchesi, J.N., Plumb, J.M., Adams, N.S., and Rondorf, D.W., 2006, Survival and migration behavior of juvenile salmonids at McNary Dam, 2004: Annual report prepared by U.S. Geological Survey, Cook, Washington, for the U.S. Army Corps of Engineers, Walla Walla, Washington, contract number W68SBV40271050.

Pickering, A.D., Pottinger, T.G., and Christie, P., 1982, Recovery of the brown trout, *Salmo trutta* L., from acute handling stress—A time-course study: Journal of Fish Biology, v. 20, p. 229–244.

Piper, R.G., McElwain, I.B., Orme, L.E. McCraven, J.P. Fowler, L.G., and Leonard, J.R., 1982, Fish hatchery management: Washington, D.C., U.S. Fish and Wildlife Service, 517 p.

Portz, D.E., Woodley, C.M., and Cech, J.J. Jr., 2006, Stress-associated impacts of short-term holding on fishes: Reviews in Fish Biology and Fisheries, v. 16, p. 25–170.

Ross, L.G., and Ross, B., 2008, Anesthetic and sedative techniques for aquatic animals (3d ed.): Oxford, United Kingdom, Blackwell Science Ltd., 222 p.

Ross, M.J., and Kleiner, C.F., 1982, Shielded needle technique for surgically implanting radio-frequency transmitters in fish: The Progressive Fish-Culturist, v. 44, p. 41–43.

Sakaris, P.C., Jesien, R.V., and Pinkey, A.E., 2005, Retention of surgically implanted ultrasonic transmitters in the Brown Bullhead Catfish: North American Journal of Fisheries Management, v. 25, p. 822–826.

San Joaquin River Group Authority, 2008, 2007 annual technical report on implementation and monitoring of the San Joaquin River Agreement and the Vernalis Adaptive Management Plan: Prepared for the California Water Resource Control Board in compliance with D-1641, January 2008, 128 p.

San Joaquin River Group Authority 2009, 2008 annual technical report on implementation and monitoring of the San Joaquin River Agreement and the Vernalis Adaptive Management Plan: Prepared for the California Water Resource Control Board in compliance with D-1641, January 2009, 128 p.

Schnick, R.A., 2006, Zero withdrawal anesthetic for all finfish and shellfish—Need and candidates: Fisheries, v. 31, p. 122–126.

Slatter, D.H., ed., 2003, Textbook of small animal surgery (3d ed.), 2 volumes: Philadelphia, Saunders, 2,712 p.

Smith, J.M., Mather, M.E., Frank, H.J., Muth, R.M., Finn, J.T., and McCormick, S.D., 2009, Evaluation of a gastric radio tag insertion technique for anadromous river herring: North American Journal of Fisheries Management, v. 29, p. 367–377.

Soivio, A., Nyholm, K., and Huhti, M., 1977, Effects of anesthesia with MS 222, neutralized MS 222, and benzocaine on the blood constituents of rainbow trout, *Salmo gairdneri*: Journal of Fish Biology, v. 10, p. 97–101.

Stasko, A.B., and Pincock, D.G., 1977, Review of underwater biotelemetry, with emphasis on ultrasonic techniques: Journal of the Fisheries Research Board of Canada, v. 34, p. 1,261–1,285.

Stickney, R.R., and Kohler, C.C., 1990, Maintaining fish for research and testing, *in* Schreck, C.B., and Moyle, P.B., eds., Methods for fish biology: Bethesda, Maryland, American Fisheries Society, p. 633–663.

Strange, R.J., and Schreck, C.B., 1978, Anesthetic and handling stress on survival and cortisol concentration in yearling Chinook salmon (*Oncorhynchus tshawytscha*): Journal of the Fisheries Research Board of Canada, v. 35, p. 345–349.

Summerfelt, R.C., and Smith, L.S., 1990, Anesthesia, surgery, and related techniques, *in* Schreck, C.B., and Moyle, P.B., eds., Methods for fish biology: Bethesda, Maryland, American Fisheries Society, p. 213–272.

Thorstad, E.B., Økland, F., and Heggberget, T.G., 2001, Are long term negative effects from external tags underestimated?—Fouling of an externally attached telemetry transmitter: Journal of Fish Biology, v. 59, p. 1,092–1,094.

Wagner, G.N., and Cooke, S.J., 2005, Methodological approaches and opinions of researchers involved in the surgical implantation of telemetry transmitters in fish: Journal of Aquatic Animal Health, v. 17, p. 160–169.

Wedemeyer, G., 1970, Stress of anesthesia with M.S. 222 and benzocaine in rainbow trout (*Salmo gairdneri*): Journal of the Fisheries Research Board of Canada, v.37, p. 909–914.

Wedemeyer, G.A., Barton, A.B., and McLeay, D.J., 1990, Stress and acclimation, *in* Schreck, C.B., and Moyle, P.B., eds., Methods for fish biology: Bethesda, Maryland, American Fisheries Society, p. 451–489.

Winter, J.D., 1996, Advances in underwater biotelemetry, *in* Murphy, B.R., and Willis, D.W., eds., Fisheries techniques (2d ed.): Bethesda, Maryland, American Fisheries Society, p. 555–590.

Zale, A.V., Brooke, C., and Fraser, W.C., 2005, Effects of surgically implanted transmitter weights on growth and swimming stamina of small adult Westslope cutthroat trout: Transactions of the American Fisheries Society, v. 134, p. 653–660.

Appendix A: Materials Needed

A list of materials is provided for study planning. The study design and numbers of fish to be tagged will dictate the quantities of materials needed and will be determined on an individual study basis. Our materials list is divided into equipment (non-expendable items) and supplies (expendable items). In some cases, there are specific recommendations for materials or the number of items needed based on our experience. In most cases, however, materials are described in general terms and can be substituted with equivalent materials as needed.

We provide some guidance on the amount of supplies to purchase, based on the number of fish to be tagged (table A1). Using the number of fish to be tagged to estimate supply needs is simplistic, however, because needs will vary depending on the number of tagging sessions, the number of fish tagged each session, the environmental conditions, and the number and experience of the taggers. For example, experienced taggers will generally use less suture material per fish than novice taggers. Some supplies, like chlorhexidine and MS-222® are needed in similar quantities whether a single fish or 25 fish are being tagged. Table A1 can be used as a broad planning guide for materials and supplies, and planning can be refined using the specific details for a given study. We encourage researchers to order supplies to accommodate practice surgeries in addition to the supplies needed for the execution of the study.

Equipment

- Digital thermometer
- Dissolved oxygen meter
- Total dissolved gas meter (depending on study conditions)
- Dark-colored 19-L containers marked with 10-L volume line and labeled "Anesthesia"
- Dark-colored 19-L containers perforated to hold 7 L of water in reservoir
- Dark-colored 19-L containers labeled "Reject"
- Dark-colored lids to fit 19-L containers
- Bench, shelf, or platform to hold gravity feed containers 45–60 cm above work platform
- Two gravity feed buckets or carboys, each marked with 10-L volume. One will be labeled "Sedation" and one will be labeled "Fresh Water" (see fig. 3)
- Tubing to connect the two gravity feed containers to each other and to the work platform, with in-line valves to allow flow from each container individually, and from both containers simultaneously (see fig. 3)
- Scale that measures weight to the nearest 0.1 g, with calibration weight
- Smooth surface measuring board with a ruler in millimeters
- Surgical table or platform to hold fish with ventral surface exposed and allow gills to be perfused. A block of closed-cell foam with a groove cut out or an acrylic glass "V" are recommended options (see fig. 1 and fig. 2)
- Dip nets
- Sanctuary nets: modified dip nets with non-porous material in deepest part of the net to retain water and allow fish to be moved without exposure to air
- Trays (n=6–8) to hold transmitters and instruments during disinfection and rinse procedures (approximately 20 cm x 10–15 cm and about 5 cm deep) (see fig. 4)

- Surgical instruments: need 4–6 complete sets of instruments per tagger to allow for rotation
  - Needle holders/drivers: recommend 12 cm Olsen-Hegar combination with scissors
  - Forceps: recommend micro dissection with 0.5–0.8 mm serrated tip
  - Micro scalpel handle (if using disposable micro scalpel blade tips)
- Small toothbrush to scrub surgical instruments
- Autoclave or pressure cooker to sterilize instruments
- Timers (count-down or count-up): water resistant timers are recommended
- Transmitters and any required activation or validation equipment (for example, receivers, hydrophones, antennas)

Supplies

- Distilled or deionized water
- Chlorhexidine diacetate solution (diluted to 30 mL/L); (Brand name: Nolvasan® by Fort Dodge)
- Tricaine methanesulfonate (MS-222®) solution (100 g/L) in an amber bottle to prevent reduction of activity due to photosensitivity
- Sodium bicarbonate (baking soda) solution (100 g/L)
- Stress Coat® (Aquarium Pharmaceuticals Inc.) or similar product: undiluted solution and 25 percent solution in squirt bottles
- Virkon® Aquatic Solution (Western Chemical); 1 percent solution in spray bottle
- 10 ml plastic syringes or graduated cylinders for dispensing solutions
- Oxygen cylinder, regulator, tubing, and airstones
- Battery-powered aerators (equipped with tubing and airstones)
- Medical-grade exam gloves (non-latex): a variety of sizes to fit all personnel
- Large plastic weigh boats (~12 cm square)
- Surgical supplies:
  - Disposable 3 mm and/or 5 mm micro scalpels with 15 degree blade angle (disposable blades or full disposable scalpels)
  - 4–0 and/or 5–0 Ethicon Vicryl Plus® sutures with RB-1 tapered needle
  - Catheters (20 gauge, 8–10 cm long); for radio transmitter implantation only
- Sharps container for disposal of needles and scalpel blades (one per tagging station)
- Autoclave bags and/or tape and towels to wrap instruments

Table A1. Estimated materials needed to tag between 10 and 100 fish.

Material	Unit multiplier	10 fish	25 fish	50 fish	100 fish
Chlorhexidine (undiluted)	2.4 ml/fish	24 ml	60 ml	120 ml	240 ml
MS-222® (powder)	0.13 g/fish	1 g	3 g	7 g	13 g
Sodium bicarbonate (powder)	0.13 g/fish	1 g	3 g	7 g	13 g
Stress Coat® (undiluted)	0.53 ml/fish	5 ml	13 ml	27 ml	53 ml
Virkon® Aquatic (powder)	5 g/tag date	5 g	5 g	10 g	20 g
Exam gloves	0.13 gloves/fish	2 gloves	4 gloves	8 gloves	14 gloves
Microscalpels	0.22 blades/fish	2 blades	6 blades	11 blades	22 blades
Suture packets	0.33 pkts/fish	4 pkts	9 pkts	17 pkts	33 pkts
Catheters	0.25/fish	3 catheters	7 catheters	13 catheters	25 catheters

Appendix B: Abbreviated Procedures

Fish Collection, Holding and Transport

1. Collect study fish using the least destructive and least stressful method that is effective.
    A. Fish that obviously are injured, diseased, or excessively burdened by pathogens should not be retained for tagging.
    B. Document the number of fish collected, but not retained, as well as the rationale used for rejection (for example, injury or disease).
2. The pre-tag holding period for a group of fish begins once fish are in the care of the researcher and ends when surgical procedures begin.
    A. The pre-tag holding period should be between 12 and 36 hours and ideally 24 hours.
    B. Record the time the pre-tag holding period begins for each container of fish.
    C. Fish should not have access to commercial fish feed during the pre-tag holding period.
3. Hold fish in containers with lids to reduce disturbance and fish loss due to jumping.
    A. Pre-tag holding densities should not exceed 20 g of fish per L of water (Formula: [mean fish wt (g) x number of fish]/L of water is less than or equal to 20 g/L).
    B. If multiple species are collected they should be held in separate, but comparable containers.
4. Monitor and maintain water-quality during pre-tag holding (and any required transport process).
    A. Dissolved oxygen concentration (DO) in pre-tag holding containers should be between 80 – 130 percent saturation.
    B. Do not transfer fish between water sources until the difference in water temperature between the sources is less than or equal to 2°C.
    C. Total dissolved gas (TDG) in pre-tag holding containers should not exceed 110 percent saturation.
5. Monitor fish behavior and condition during pre-tag holding (or at a minimum, prior to tagging).
6. Transport of untagged or tagged fish should be designed to minimize stress to fish.
    A. Monitor and maintain water-quality parameters established for fish holding.
    B. If water temperature rises significantly during transport, the addition of ice may be required. Be aware that most commercially produced ice contains chlorine, which may be harmful to fish.
    C. Select a transport route of travel for the shortest and smoothest ride to minimize jarring.

Fish Size Criteria

1. The weight of the transmitter in air must not exceed 5 percent of the weight of the fish in air.

Tagging Preparations

1. Monitor and maintain water-quality in all fish containers before, during, and after the tagging session.
    A. DO should be between 80 – 130 percent saturation in all water sources that hold fish.

B. TDG should be less than 110 percent in all water sources that hold fish.

C. Do not transfer fish between water sources until the water temperature difference is less than or equal to 2°C.

2. Prepare tagging equipment and supplies.

   A. Confirm specifications (that is, frequency, pulse rate, and so on) and operation of transmitters, and/or PIT tags.

   B. Disinfect and rinse transmitters.

      i. Immerse transmitters in chlorhexidine solution for 15 minutes.
      ii. Thoroughly rinse transmitters in distilled or deionized water.
      iii. Following disinfection, handle transmitters only with clean instruments or clean, gloved hands.

   C. Prepare the tagging station.

      i. Set up the irrigation system (gravity feed or pump).
      ii. Pour chlorhexidine solution into disinfection trays.
      iii. Pour distilled or deionized water into a rinse tray.
      iv. Put tagging supplies (that is, sutures and blades) near the tagging station, and load each tray with a complete set of sterile surgical instruments.

   D. Prepare the measuring board and scale.

      i. Measuring board should be made of smooth material and in good condition.
      ii. Ensure that the scale is functioning, and calibrated regularly.
      iii. Place a plastic weigh boat on the pan of the scale.
      iv. Wet the measuring board and weigh boat with diluted Stress Coat® solution.

3. Prepare recovery containers.

   A. Fill recovery containers with source water just prior to the start of tagging to maintain optimal water-quality.

   B. DO concentration in recovery containers should be between 120 – 150 percent saturation.

   C. Fish density in recovery containers should not exceed 10 g of fish per L of water.

   D. Position containers near the tagging station.

4. Prepare a reject container.

   A. Fill reject container(s) with source water just prior to start of tagging to maintain optimal water-quality.

   B. Equip the container with a battery-operated aerator.

   C. Position the container near the tagging station.

5. Prepare anesthesia.

   A. Prepare the anesthesia container.

      i. Fill the 19-L anesthesia container with 10 L of source water and add MS-222® stock solution.
      ii. For each mL of MS-222® stock solution added to the container, add the same amount of sodium bicarbonate stock solution.
      iii. Add approximately 10 mL of diluted Stress Coat® solution to the container.

ＩＶ. Cover the anesthesia bucket with a lid, place a timer on the lid, and position the container near the source of fish to be tagged.

B. Prepare gravity feed containers.

    i. Fill both gravity feed containers with 10-L of source water. Add 2 mL of MS-222® stock solution and 2 mL of sodium bicarbonate stock solution to the sedation container.

    ii. Place both containers on an elevated platform and connect tubing between the containers and the tagging platform.

Anesthetizing Fish

1. Net one fish from the pre-tag holding container and place directly into the anesthesia container.

    A. Immediately place a lid on the container.

    B. Start a timer to document the MS-222® exposure time.

2. Remove the lid after approximately 1 minute to monitor the stage of anesthesia.

    A. Induction time should be 2-4 minutes, with an average time of 3 minutes.

    B. If a fish loses equilibrium in less than 1 minute it should not be tagged.

    C. Net the fish from the anesthesia container into the Reject container.

3. Once the fish loses equilibrium examine the fish for condition.

    A. Keep the fish submerged during the examination.

    B. Look for marks, tags, clips, fungus, descaling, injury, parasites, and signs of disease.

    C. Fish that are not acceptable for tagging should be transferred to the Reject container.

4. Wait 30–60 seconds after the fish has lost equilibrium to remove it from anesthesia.

    A. Use a net or gloved hand to remove the fish.

    B. Start a timer to monitor the air exposure time.

    C. Note the anesthesia exposure time.

    D. Fish exposed to MS-222® for 5 minutes or longer should be rejected.

5. Monitor anesthesia for several fish and adjust concentration as needed.

    A. Adjust concentration (up or down) in 5 mg/L increments of working concentration (or 0.5 mL increments of stock solution).

    B. Note any change of anesthesia on the datasheet.

    C. Anesthetize another group of fish and monitor the new concentration for effectiveness.

    D. If more than one tagger is operating, coordinate the change of concentration so that it applies to all taggers.

6. Add anesthesia containers as needed to minimize delays, keeping a single fish in each container, with a separate timer.

Measuring Fish Size

1. Transfer fish from the anesthesia bucket to a measuring board.

    A. Ensure that a timer is started to measure air exposure time.

    B. Measure and record fork length (FL) to the nearest millimeter.

C. The FL is the distance from the snout to the fork in the caudal fin.

D. Regularly add diluted Stress Coat® to keep the surface of the board wet.

2. Transfer the fish to the weigh boat on the scale.

   A. Tare the scale so that it shows zero with the weigh boat and Stress Coat® added.

   B. Measure and record weight to the nearest 0.1 g.

   C. Regularly add diluted Stress Coat® to keep weigh boat wet.

3. Make all transfers by cradling fish in two hands.

   A. If a fish is dropped to the floor before it is tagged it must be rejected.

   B. If a fish is dropped on the tagging surface it may be repositioned and tagged at the tagger's discretion.

   C. If a fish is dropped to the floor after it is tagged it should be euthanized, and the transmitter should be removed, disinfected, and used in another fish.

4. Vocally relay fish size data to a recorder to speed fish handling and ensure data accuracy.

Implantation of Transmitters

1. Place the fish on the surgery platform ventral side up and establish irrigation.

   A. Place the gravity feed tubing into the mouth of the fish.

      i. Deliver sedation water from the sedation gravity feed container.

      ii. Ensure water flow over the gills; adjust flow using the valves.

      iii. Inadequate flow will cause the fish to become agitated.

      iv. Recline the head of the fish to avoid water entering the body cavity through the incision.

   B. Lighten the sedation dose as the surgery progresses to begin recovery.

      i. At the mid-point of the surgery consider providing a mix of freshwater and sedation.

      ii. Near the end of the surgery try to provide completely freshwater irrigation.

2. Conduct a second external exam to evaluate fish condition and determine suitability for tagging.

   A. Briefly examine fully anesthetized fish now that it is out of the water.

   B. Record fish condition notes.

3. Use a micro scalpel to make an incision.

   A. In general use a 5 mm blade for fish that weigh more than about 50 g and a 3 mm blade for smaller fish.

      i. The choice of micro scalpel blade will depend on the thickness of the body wall.

      ii. Blade selection should be done through experimentation.

   B. Locate the pelvic girdle of the fish by visual exam and palpation.

      i. In a ventral view the pelvic girdle has a "V" or "U" shape.

      ii. The most anterior point of the pelvic girdle is the positioning guide.

   C. Make an incision about 3 mm anterior to the anterior point of the pelvic girdle, and about 3 mm away from and parallel to the mid-ventral line .

      i. Draw the blade toward the head of the fish.

    ii.   The incision should be only long enough to allow insertion of the transmitter without tearing the adjacent tissue.

    iii.   The incision should be deep enough to penetrate the peritoneum without damaging internal organs.

    iv.   The incision would ideally be made with a single pass of the micro scalpel.

    v.   One micro scalpel blade can be used on several fish before it becomes dull.

4. Use forceps to open the incision and quickly evaluate any potential organ damage.

   A. Insert forceps to ensure that the peritoneum was penetrated along the full length of the incision.

   B. Assess any potential organ damage by looking for bleeding.

   C. If the fish is bleeding excessively it should not be implanted with a transmitter.

5. If the transmitter has an external antenna, make an antenna exit site in the lateral body wall using a modified shielded needle technique. If the transmitter has no external antenna, proceed to step 6.

   A. A plastic catheter, positioned over a needle, is termed a "shielded needle" (see fig. 10).

   B. Following purchase, the catheter typically must be modified slightly to function as a shield.

   C. Insert the shielded needle through the incision and guide it to the antenna exit site.

    i.   Keep the needle tip covered by the catheter to protect the organs.

    ii.   The antenna exit site should be even with the insertion of the pelvic fins and about 40 percent of the distance from the mid-ventral line to the lateral line (see fig. 11).

   D. Once positioned at the antenna exit site, use the needle to puncture the body wall.

    i.   The cutting edge of the needle should be facing away from the body wall (see fig. 12).

    ii.   Puncture the body wall with the needle, not the catheter.

    iii.   Advance the catheter through the wound until it is visible from the outside of the fish.

   E. Hold the catheter in position, extending out the incision and the exit wound, and withdraw the needle.

    i.   In this position the catheter forms a channel for the transmitter antenna.

    ii.   Select the catheter with the smallest diameter that will accommodate the transmitter antenna and is of appropriate length.

    iii.   A single needle can be used for several surgeries.

   F. Route the transmitter antenna through the catheter, starting at the incision.

    i.   Keep the body of the transmitter in your gloved hand.

    ii.   Pull the catheter out of the body wall and off the antenna.

6. Insert the transmitter into the abdominal cavity.

   A. Orient the transmitter so that the top or bottom is inserted first.

   B. Carefully insert the transmitter through the incision.

   C. Position the transmitter directly beneath the incision.

   D. If additional tags (for example, PIT tags) will be used insert them through the incision.

7. Close the incision with sutures.

    A. Two sutures, in a simple interrupted pattern, are used to close the incision.

        i. The simple interrupted pattern involves independent closure efforts.

        ii. Use a modified surgeon's (or friction) knot to secure each suture.

        iii. Suture entry and exit sites should be approximately 2 mm from the incision edge.

    B. A third suture may be added if needed to adequately close the incision.

        i. Position sutures so that there is an approximately equal distance between the sutures and between the sutures and the anterior and posterior edges of the incision (see fig. 13).

        ii. Adding a third suture poses some risks but is warranted if there is risk of transmitter loss due to a partially open incision.

        iii. Note on the datasheet the addition of a third suture.

    C. There is no exact specification on suture size.

        i. Use the smallest diameter suture material that will secure the incision without tearing through the adjacent tissue.

        ii. Typically a 4–0 suture is used for fish that weigh about 50 g and a 5–0 suture is used for smaller fish.

        iii. A single suture packet is used for several fish and must be disinfected and rinsed between fish surgeries, following the same procedures as for instruments.

8. Switch irrigation water from sedation to freshwater.

    A. The ventilation rate of the fish must be monitored throughout the procedure.

    B. Irrigation should be switched to freshwater to begin the recovery from anesthesia.

    C. Sedation can be continued for active fish.

9. Rotate surgical instruments and suture material to ensure adequate disinfection.

    A. Multiple sets of instruments must be available.

    B. Gently place micro scalpel blades into the disinfectant bath to avoid damaging delicate blades.

    C. Organic debris should be removed from instruments before disinfection.

    D. Replace the chlorhexidine in the disinfectant trays to maintain efficacy.

    E. Rotate unused portions of suture with a set of instruments.

    F. Replace the water in the rinse tray as needed to ensure adequate rinsing.

10. Record any special conditions that occurred during the procedure for an individual fish.

Post-Tag Recovery

1. Monitor the water-quality in recovery containers and make any needed adjustments.

    A. The temperature of the containers should be less than 2°C different from the water source.

    B. The DO concentration in the containers should be 120–150 percent saturation.

    C. TDG should not exceed 110 percent saturation.

2. Transfer fish from the surgery platform to a recovery container.

    A. Hold the fish in position on the surgery platform and carry the platform to the recovery container to reduce the risk of dropping fish.

    B. Cover the container immediately after the fish enters.

C. Stop the timer that records the air exposure time and note the time on the datasheet.

D. The density in recovery containers should not exceed 10 g of fish per L of water.

E. Start a timer to record the minimum recovery time for fish in a given recovery container.

    i. Monitor fish for short-term recovery before transferring them to a post-tag holding container.

    ii. Tagged fish should remain in recovery containers for at least 10 minutes to ensure access to high DO saturation.

    iii. Monitor fish for recovery of equilibrium.

F. Fish that take more than about 5 minutes to regain equilibrium require close monitoring.

    i. Manually ram ventilate fish with slow recovery. Move the fish forward and back within the recovery container.

    ii. Tagged fish that do not recover should be euthanized.

G. Transfer fish to the post-tag holding container.

Post-Tag Holding and Fish Release

1. Configure post-tag holding to reduce fish transfers and facilitate release.

A. Hold fish using a system where the small, mobile containers used for recovery can be used for post-tag holding.

B. Post-tag holding should be configured so that tagged fish can be released without a net transfer.

2. Allow tagged fish access to the air-water interface throughout the post-tag holding period.

3. The post-tag holding density should not exceed 10 g of fish per L of water.

4. The post-tag holding period should be 18–36 hours, and optimally about 24 hours.

A. The holding period begins when the last fish is placed into the post-tag holding container.

B. The holding period ends when fish are removed in preparation for transport or release.

5. Maintain water-quality in post-tag holding containers.

A. Water temperatures should be maintained within approximately 2°C of the tagging or release water source.

B. DO concentrations should be near 100 percent saturation.

C. TDG should not exceed 110 percent saturation.

6. Examine fish to assess condition before release.

A. Visually examine fish with as little disturbance as possible.

    i. Partially remove the lid of the container to visualize fish.

    ii. Observe fish condition (for example, swimming activity and/or vertical position).

B. Carefully remove moribund, dead, or poorly performing fish, minimizing disturbance to the remaining fish.

7. Release the tagged fish.

    A. Ensure transmitter function following surgery and water exposure.

    B. Compare water temperatures in the post-tag holding container and at the release location.

        i. If the temperatures are more than 2°C different, mix the water sources until the difference is less than 2°C.

        ii. Tempering should occur at a rate of 0.5°C/15 minutes.

    C. Maintain water-quality and access to the air-water interface during any required transport.

        i. Maintain the water temperature in transport containers within 2°C of the release location.

        ii. Use insulated containers, a refrigerated transport truck, or non-chlorinated ice to prevent significant temperature increases.

        iii. Document water temperature during transport with a thermograph.

        iv. Maintain access to the air-water interface during transport.

    D. Let tagged fish volitionally swim out of the release container.

    E. Record release time for individual tagged fish or groups.

Clean-Up and Disinfection

1. Release, return, or euthanize rejected fish and source fish that were not needed for tagging.

2. Discard tagging solutions following local guidance.

3. Clean surgical instruments and prepare them for the next tagging operation.

    A. Remove all micro scalpel blades and dispose of them in a sharps container.

    B. Discard any partially used suture packets in a sharps container.

    C. If catheters were used, discard the plastic catheter as it cannot be sterilized.

    D. Use a small toothbrush to scrub organic debris off of all surgical instruments.

    E. Wrap instruments in a cloth or place them into an autoclave bag with autoclave tape.

    F. Sterilize instruments in an autoclave and confirm appropriate temperature exposure by visualizing a color change in the autoclave tape or bags.

4. Disinfect all working surfaces and equipment.

    A. Spray countertops, the tagging platform, and any other working surfaces with Virkon® Aquatic. Allow 10 minutes of contact time and rinse with clean water.

    B. Disinfect all water containers regularly. Spray the containers with Virkon® Aquatic, allow 10 minutes of contact time, and rinse with clean water.

5. Clean and disinfect pre-tag and post-tag holding containers regularly.

6. Allow a thorough drying period for all equipment.

Appendix C: SOP Compliance Form

Tagging Procedures SOP Compliance Inspection

Tagger: _____

Crew: _____

Inspector: _____

Date: _____

Time: _____

1. Were fish held 12 to 36 hours prior to tagging?

[ ] Yes   [ ] No   [ ] Did not observe

_____ date and time tagging started

_____ date and time last fish were delivered

_____ difference = pre-tag hold time

Corrective action (if applicable):

2. Were fish held at appropriate densities?
for pre-tag holding: ((mean fish weight(g)) x (number of fish) / (L of water) less than or equal to 20g/L

[ ] Yes   [ ] No   [ ] Did not observe

Comments:

Corrective action (if applicable):

3. Were transmitters checked to ensure that they were operating prior to implantation?

[ ] Yes   [ ] No   [ ] Did not observe

Comments:

Corrective action (if applicable):

46

Tagging Procedures SOP Compliance Inspection—Continued

4. Were water containers filled with water immediately prior to tagging to prevent loss of water quality?

☐ Yes   ☐ No   ☐ Did not observe

Comments:

Corrective action (if applicable):

5. Were transmitters disinfected in chlorhexidine and rinsed prior to implantation?

☐ Yes   ☐ No   ☐ Did not observe

Comments:

Corrective action (if applicable):

6. Were MS-222® and bicarbonate added to the anesthesia containers resulting in the proper concentration?

☐ Yes   ☐ No   ☐ Did not observe

Comments:

Corrective action (if applicable):

7. Was Stress Coat® used appropriately on surfaces and in containers?

☐ Yes   ☐ No   ☐ Did not observe

Comments:

Corrective action (if applicable):

Tagging Procedures SOP Compliance Inspection—Continued

8. Were sanctuary nets used for netting fish? Was care taken to minimize chasing?

☐ Yes ☐ No ☐ Did not observe

Comments:

Corrective action (if applicable):

9. Were lids used on all containers holding fish?

☐ Yes ☐ No ☐ Did not observe

Comments:

Corrective action (if applicable):

10. Did staff ensure that all fish in a recovery container had regained equilibrium before moving them to post-tag holding containers?

☐ Yes ☐ No ☐ Did not observe

Comments:

Corrective action (if applicable):

11. For dissolved oxygen (DO) and temperature measurements using a YSI-55:

Was the meter on for 15 minutes prior to calibration? ☐ Yes ☐ No ☐ Did not observe

Was the meter calibrated? ☐ Yes ☐ No ☐ Did not observe

Were measurements taken correctly? ☐ Yes ☐ No ☐ Did not observe

(that is, Was the probe continuously moved? Did the values stabilize before being recorded?)

Comments:

Corrective action (if applicable):

Tagging Procedures SOP Compliance Inspection—Continued

12. Were the following water-quality measurements taken:

Temp and DO before tagging in the pre-tag holding area   ☐ Yes   ☐ No   ☐ Did not observe

Temp and DO after tagging in river near holding containers   ☐ Yes   ☐ No   ☐ Did not observe

Temp and DO in recovery buckets   ☐ Yes   ☐ No   ☐ Did not observe

Comments:

Corrective action (if applicable):

13. If water-quality measurements were outside the acceptable range, was corrective action taken?

☐ Yes   ☐ No   ☐ Did not observe   ☐ Readings were within acceptable range

Comments:

Corrective action (if applicable):

14. Were all datasheets filled out correctly?

☐ Yes   ☐ No   ☐ Did not observe

Comments:

Corrective action (if applicable):